THE **FASHION** FILE

THE FASHION FILE

Advice, tips and inspiration from the costume designer of **MAD MEN**

Janie Bryant with Monica Corcoran Harel

FOREWORD BY JANUARY JONES

Illustrations by Robert Best

APPLE

First published in the UK in 2011 by

Apple Press
7 Greenland Street
London NW1 0ND

www.apple-press.com

First US Edition: November 2010

ISBN 978 1 84543 402 1

Designed by Hoffman Creative
For photography credits and copyright information, see page 171.

Jacket Copyright Hachette Book Group, Inc
Printed in Singapore
Cover design by Hoffman Creative
Cover illustrations by Robert Best

This book is dedicated...

To my childhood babysitter Karen McKinley Smith who helped
me make my first dress at the age of 8. To my Mom who always
taught me the importance of being a lady and so much more.
To my Gran Gran who shared my love of roses, dolls, beauty,
and fashion. And to Monica, my style mate.

—Janie

To my hero and husband, Gadi. And to Janie B.,
for countless cups of tea and the many laughs along the way.

—Monica

CONTENTS

» *It's a huge cheat as an actor to be able to go to the set in the morning in your jeans and then get in your costume.*

FOREWORD
by JANUARY JONES

I remember my first fitting with Janie for *Mad Men*. I had just had a long conversation with executive producer Mathew Weiner about the role of Betty, and how she was going to be in therapy and have physical issues as a result of her anxiety, and it was all very daunting and new for me. So when I walked in for my fitting I was panicking a bit about portraying such a complex character. But Janie's enthusiasm and passion for the clothes and the time period helped renew my own passion and, after seeing all of Betty's wardrobe, I trusted Janie completely. We bonded in our mutual respect for fashion and storytelling through the amazing '60s garments she uses on the show.

As an actor playing a role in a period piece, it's a big cheat to arrive on set each day in your every-day clothes and, an hour and a half later, be transformed by hair, makeup, and wardrobe. And Janie doesn't leave anything out. From the girdle, long-line bras, stockings, and petticoats, you feel like a different person before ever uttering a line. All those elements contribute to making me feel, walk, and posture as Betty.

Janie gets very emotional when everything comes together. On occasion I have had to plead with her not to cry when she's seen the finished result. It's so inspiring to see someone care that much about her work and the real art that is what she does. On a show as stylized as *Mad Men* that's important to the honesty of the storytelling and to the actors. There have been very few times I've questioned her judgment, but when I have, she's just said in her delicate

» *In my personal life, I like to take risks with all kinds of different fashions. I don't think I have a specific style. Every day I wake up and dress the part, which is fun.*

January Jones on the red carpet at the 2010 Golden Globes.

Southern accent, "January, you're going to love it. Just wait!" And I always do.

I think one of the hugest compliments to Janie's work on *Mad Men* is how it has inspired modern fashion. Michael Kors was one of the first to come out with a *Mad Men*–inspired collection. We're suddenly seeing a waistline again and the silhouettes of the '50s and early '60s. I'm happily surprised to see women dressing like women again; a feminine tribute through tailoring.

» I'm always most excited to see what Janie's going to wear. She can take pieces from any decade and make them look modern.

A vintage gold bracelet with porcelain flowers, given to Janie by January.

Janie is a firm believer that you don't have to spend a lot of money to look fabulous. You can find something vintage and alter it and make it really special. I'm always excited to see what Janie's wearing. You can't pinpoint her style because it's different every day, but modernizing a garment from any decade, whether it be with accessories or just the look in her eye, is her gift. She nails it every time.

I have learned from Janie to take risks in what I wear. I can't say I have a specific style, I just know which silhouettes compliment my frame. My advice is to just make sure you wear it and that the garment doesn't wear you. Finding something special and unique in a vintage store has become a sport for me. Even if a piece may seem a bit outlandish, as long as you feel confident and beautiful in it, it's a risk worth taking

Thank you, Janie Bryant, for inspiring not only me, but the world over with your dedication to fashion and storytelling.

INTRODUCTION:
STEP INSIDE
my FITTING
ROOM

When I was five years old and growing up in Tennessee, all I wanted to do was wear high heels. It was my dream. The first time I played dress-up, I slipped into my mother's black patent-leather pumps and her full-length black slip with the lace bodice. Very Elizabeth Taylor of me. I topped it off and accessorized with a sixties floral mod cap with a ruffle brim and big white sunglasses. Never mind that I could stride in two-inch heels like a lady. Even back then, the transformative power of a costume awed me.

Nowadays, that magical metamorphosis consumes my day-to-day life as a costume designer. My process on *Mad Men* always starts with a script, which I read several times to get a sense of the characters' dialogue, color palette, and silhouette. Someone as fiery as Joan Holloway, for instance, will wear mostly bold, solid jewel tones like emerald green and purple. Peggy Olson, who's more perky and complex, gets a parochial wardrobe of plaids and pleats.

Once I've made some notes, I research old photos to get a better image of the time period. Shots of Cary Grant and Gregory Peck help inspire Don Draper's look, while Marilyn Monroe and Sophia Loren are models for

Joan. Next I sketch the ensembles and add hue with watercolors. My cutter-fitter drapes the muslin on the dress forms and then creates paper patterns, which eventually create the shape of the fabrics that are cut and sewn into the actual pencil skirts, cocktail dresses, and suits.

Now it's time to schedule fittings. On a regular day on the set of *Mad Men,* the costume crew and I can fit dozens of people. The actors saunter into the fitting room wearing contemporary clothes and makeup. It's my job to transport these actors back to another era and help them become their characters. How to turn a fitting room into a time machine? My secret weapon for the women is a cache of undergarments, from closed-bottom girdles with garters to lacy bullet brassieres. These foundations affect how the characters walk, sit, and sigh, and the transformation begins with that first breath.

For the leading ladies like January Jones, who plays Betty, I don't just create a look scene by scene; I need to know what Betty will be doing throughout the season so she has the right outfit for any situation. What will she wear as she lounges at home or heads off to a swank cocktail soirée? How about a frock for hosting a dinner party? I create a whole closet for her that includes day dresses, evening wear, sweater sets, trousers, and peignoirs for all seasons. *Mad Men* creator and executive producer Matt Weiner calls it "unwrapping the package" to get to a character. I call it "peeling the onion."

Whether I'm creating looks for Betty or Joan, there is that moment when the clothes make the character. It just clicks. Maybe it's the sharkskin suit that creates Don's debonair silhouette. Or the frothy silk cocktail dress that makes Betty stand out as a woman who longs for admiration. It could be Joan's fitted crepe-wool sheath that announces her every asset. The actor looks in the mirror and says, "Thank you. Now I know who I am."

» *Knowing your "character" is the key to cultivating your style. Who do you want to be today? With the right clothes, you can be whomever you want to be. And you can change your "character" from day to day, depending on your needs and whims.*

That transformation works outside the *Mad Men* fitting room, too. Knowing your "character" is the key to cultivating your style. Who do you want to be today? Straight-forward or mysterious? Demure like Betty or commanding like Joan? Defining your intention and the image you want to cultivate is the first step to honing your style. With the right clothes, you can be whomever you want to be. And you can change your "character" from day to day, depending on your needs and whims.

Now it's *your* turn to step inside my fitting room.

*Me, browsing through
the 1960s cocktail dresses
at Palace Costumes.*

You as a
LEADING
LADY

1

Clearly, a leading lady always stands out in a crowd. She's that regal white rose amidst a bouquet of plucky pink tulips or a flash of sexy black lace against a backdrop of pale blue brocade. Take Joan Holloway. You would never mistake her for just another typist in the secretary pool. Betty Draper, too, always shanghais a scene, whether she's swanning at a black-tie gala or just swapping gossip with her girlfriends.

My job is to make sure that these women never blend in or get eclipsed by another character. Sure, Joan has a collision-causing figure and Betty's angelic features evoke awe. But without their signature styles these gorgeous women would surely recede a bit into the background.

For example, Joan is well aware of her bewitching curves and never misses out on an opportunity to accentuate them in a form-fitting, jewel-toned sheath. She understands her assets and playfully exploits them. Betty knows that her perfect housewife image is only punctuated by a string of dainty, lustrous pearls and full-skirted dresses. She radiates domestic chic. And let's not forget darling Peggy Olson, with her Catholic schoolgirl–inspired preference for plaids, polka dots, and stripes. Peggy's clothes telegraph her go-getter spirit and ambition.

Let's explore your myriad style options, from the perfect color to the proper intention, and soon you, too, will be ready to make a grand entrance.

Your trademark look

A signature style—think of it as the way you sign your name—is one way to quickly establish a presence. It could be a preference for wearing a dramatic color like bright blue or fuchsia. Or a penchant for showing off your legs. Maybe you love the look of statement accessories like chunky, layered tribal necklaces or oversized cuffs. Any one of these style choices can become your signature. The same goes for a distinctive hairstyle or cosmetic flourish. (Think about Brigitte Bardot with her signature cat-eye makeup or Louise Brooks and her trademark bob and you get the point.)

Of course, you should never become enslaved to a signature style. Wearing purple ensembles or skirts, from pencils to minis, *all* the time could be misconstrued as an obsessive disorder. And who wants to be known as the woman in the little yellow hat? My signature style is rooted in the classics, but I am always striving to change up the mood by mixing in unique pieces from different decades. I wear my sweetheart bracelets almost every day, but I might contrast them with a mod, fitted leather dress or a faux-fur bomber jacket.

Your own signature style should always pack a subtle punch. But, most importantly, it should be an outgrowth of your personal style and not an offshoot of a current, hot trend. Once you have determined an individual accent, show it off regularly, but not constantly. What is it that inspires you?

» I wear my sweetheart bracelets almost every day, but I might contrast them with a mod, fitted leather dress or a faux-fur bomber jacket.

Sweetheart bracelets were once a popular token of courtship.

Are you a *Betty* or a *Joan?*

Getting dressed is a lot like planning a holiday abroad. It calls for some foresight, pep, and a clear road map. When I design costumes for a character, I first think: Who is this woman and what do I want to convey? Is she supposed to come across as a take-charge executive or a self-assured assistant? Would this character be bold enough to talk back to her boss or is she more the type just to silently pray for a promotion?

By finding your intentions, or goals, you create a trusty style compass. Come up with three adjectives that describe the image you want to broadcast with your look. Think of easily translatable words like "strong" or "romantic" or "elegant." When I first envisioned Don Draper, I saw him as "mysterious" and "secretive" and then created costumes that were minimal in style to suit his cryptic personality.

As I thought about Betty Draper, "perfectionist" came to mind, and I built a polished wardrobe of printed silks, petticoats, and shirtwaist dresses around her need always to look feminine and flawless. Betty often wears white because, in my opinion, she's striving to be the perpetual bride. Joan Holloway is clearly "sassy" and "sexy." Her wardrobe, from the tight sweaters and pencil skirts to the bold jeweled-tone sheaths, reflects her poise and self-possession. "Ambition" and "complexity" drive Peggy's parochial plaids and pleats.

Take a moment to think about how you would like to be perceived and what you would like to achieve today. Is it important that you look "powerful" and "capable" for a presentation? Or do you need to reveal a "sexy" and "softer" side for a first date? With a few words and an intention, you now have a direction—a purpose, even—when you gaze out at those vast choices in your closet. Again, who do you want to be today? Commit to a character. Now you won't waste time debating between the metallic bolero jacket and the houndstooth blazer. Or look down at your ballet flats during a board meeting and think, "Damn. I should have worn the power heels."

Inspiration found here

Wardrobes aren't built in a day. Just think of all the hours you have devoted to amassing your own closet. (I'll start advising you on building your wardrobe on page 56.) To create a leading lady's look, I spend hours researching in order to visualize her signature style. Old Montgomery Ward catalogs, vintage magazines like *Vogue* and *Good Housekeeping* and *Ladies' Home Journal,* advertisements and stock photographs from the 1950s and 1960s all fuel my inspiration for *Mad Men*'s costumes. I clip snapshots and even snip swatches of fabric that help me to imagine the essence of a character and her look.

After gathering my visual ammo, it's time to create an inspiration board. Costume designers can't live without them. Betty Draper's board is a collision of tear sheets from my grandmother's knitting magazines from the 1960s, candid shots of Grace Kelly, and even a picture of a pink washer and dryer. Oh—and there's a bright blue refrigerator, too. (The appliances help me get into her mind-set as a homemaker.) I have one image of Grace Kelly standing alone behind a fence, watching her children play on a swing set. She's in a perfect wool suit and wearing sunglasses. Her look reminds me so strongly of Betty's character. Fabric swatches in shades of gray and cool blues are posted to help me formulate her color palette, as well.

Even at home I keep a running inspiration board. Confession: Okay, I have more than a few, devoted to accessories, fashion, travel, and beauty. My inspirations include a picture of a music festival in Mali (I'm obsessed with visiting Africa) and a red satin Christian Louboutin clutch with a gilded frame of gold vipers.

Start cutting out images that capture the mood of how you want to look and make a collage of them on a bulletin board. One picture could be a tear sheet from a fashion magazine; another could feature a flashy color that draws your eye but you've never been daring enough to wear. Before you get dressed or go shopping for a new dress or shoes, study your inspiration board. Examine and take note of the colors and fabrics you have chosen to feature so you can seek them out. If pictures of gardens or flowers adorn your board, it's time to try on a floral print. (Or maybe a gardenia or tuberose perfume.) Be mindful of the styles that speak to you, too. If you have snipped out photos of women wearing sleek, architectural cocktail dresses, try on a square-necked sheath or a strapless column dress. These visual cues will help focus you and the style you want to create.

» *Betty Draper's board is a collision of tear sheets from my grandmother's knitting magazines from the 1960s, candid shots of Grace Kelly, and even a picture of a pink washer and dryer.*

A fur muff and a sixties wool suit: perfection.

Color me chic

Stop signs and fire trucks are red for a very good reason. If I need one of my characters to captivate a scene, she'll be costumed in a bright, bold color. Picture this: The camera pans a room filled with women outfitted in black or gray or camel and suddenly alights on the lady in a turquoise dress or a crimson silk blouse. Wham! She now owns every eyeball. Wearing a look-this-way hue, she doesn't even have to flutter her lashes or spill a drink to get noticed.

I use color to convey the inner mood of a character, too. The palette for a leading lady varies according to her attitude or emotion in each particular scene. I would never put a depressed secretary in a bold egg-yolk yellow or try to downplay a cheery housewife in a shade of pea-soup green. Her palette is a visual extension of her character development.

Ever notice how you instinctively reach for that burned-coffee-brown sweater on a day when you're feeling drab? Or how you gravitate toward a candy-colored jacket when you're soaring with endorphins? Next time you get dressed or go shopping, experiment with colors and notice how a stimulating shade like orange can actually elevate a dull mood. In fact, orange happens to be the color of creativity and enlightenment,

according to Hindu culture. Or notice how a soft, relaxing shade like pale blue or lilac can lull stress and tension.

Take a look inside your closet and make note of the most prominent hues. Are you a safe and somber dresser who opts for dark shades like black and burgundy and navy most of the time? Or a peppy risk-taker with a surplus of metallic separates and Kelly green tops? Hold a few different colored pieces up to your face and see if the palette brings out your eyes or warms your complexion. Your choice of color personifies who you are and definitely sends a message. Choose a color that makes you feel most radiant. As Coco Chanel once said, "The best color in the world is the one that looks good on you."

By the way, that seasonal palette—Are you an autumn?—actually originates in the teachings of color theorist and Bauhaus artist Johannes Itten. He saw that his students favored certain hues that complemented the tones of their complexion and hair and assigned them various seasons. (At Colormebeautiful.com, you can take a simple online quiz to find out your season and the palette that best suits you.) Read on to learn more about matching the right hues to your natural coloring.

» *Hold a few different colored pieces up to your face and see if the palette brings out your eyes or warms your complexion. Your choice of color personifies who you are and definitely sends a message.*

Your skin tone, eye and hair color all help to define your "season."
The best way to determine your complexion's undertones is to hold a sheet of white paper next to your face in a setting with natural light—and a mirror, of course.

If your hair and eyes are dark and your complexion is fair or olive with a hint of cool blue or pink undertones, you're considered a *"winter."* (Brunettes with dark brown or blue eyes and many Asian and African American women fall into this season.) Strong colors like black, navy, charcoal gray, white, and jewel tones complement your complexion.

"Summer" complexions also feature cool pink undertones, but the skin is always fair—even porcelain—and hair is usually blonde or light brown. Eyes, too, are lighter shades of brown, green, or blue. Soft blues, pinks, yellows, and greens in pastel hues work well, as do mauves, plums, and subtle blue grays.

If you're a redhead or strawberry blonde with fiery golden or yellow undertones to your skin and caramel, dark blue, or hazel eyes, you're an *"autumn."* Dark brunettes with auburn highlights are included, as well. Look for clothes with the same undertones like camel, burnt orange, peach, taupe, and copper. Off-whites like beige and cream suit you better than stark white.

"Spring" complexions are fair with warm, golden, or peach undertones, and may feature freckles and rosy or ruddy cheeks. Hair is usually strawberry blonde or light brown with extremely pale eyes. Lively colors like salmon, aqua, teal, and lime green all contrast well with your skin and hair.

HERE'S MY HANDY COLOR CHART, BASED ON HOW I COSTUME DIFFERENT CHARACTERS

Upbeat
Bright reds, vivid blues, and canary yellows. Think of the colors of fresh, ripe fruits like oranges, cherries, and bananas.

Powerful
Black, maroon, regal purple, and metallics like gold or silver. Consider colors that command and were once favored by queens.

Balancing
Pale blues and lavenders, dove grays, and light greens. Imagine colors of nature seen through a soft lens.

Intense
Fuchsia, royal blue, and bold prints like geometrics, plaids, and stripes. These shades and patterns signal a ferocity and a degree of complexity.

HOW COLOR MAKES A CHARACTER

Betty Draper	Pale blues, winter whites, camels, grays, and shades of violet epitomize Betty's glacial personality. Those colors look great with her blonde hair, blue eyes, naturally rosy lips, and fair complexion, too.
Joan Holloway	I always design costumes in jewel tones—forest green, coral, purple, teal blue, and red—for her because they reflect her strength in the office. The contrast between those deep, rich colors and her alabaster skin and red hair is amazing.
Peggy Olson	Elisabeth Moss, who plays Peggy, always begs me, "Please, no more mustard!" But I think those lackluster tones of green and yellow, which were so popular in that era, well convey her character's modesty.
Trudy Campbell	Because I envision her as a young, city version of Betty, Pete's wife wears cool sixties prints like paisleys and geometrics. She also favors optimistic shades of blue—from teal to azure—because they complement her husband's suits. I call the color "Campbell blue."

Joan and Peggy would never fight over each other's wardrobes. Each actress has her own color palette, of course.

Betty wears a white linen dress with a built-in silk polka dot sash.

The feminine factor

A waist is a terrible thing to waste. I am always amazed and saddened when I see women in shapeless, oversized T-shirts and baggy khaki pants that swallow their hips. From behind, they could easily be mistaken for teenage boys or middle-aged men. Suffice it to say, being called "sir" is anything but sexy.

Maybe one woman assumes that looking feminine requires too much work. Or another might be disenchanted with her current shape and, understandably, assumes that an oversized hoodie will disguise flaws. Not so. Completely sacrificing your feminine power and silhouette strictly for ease or camouflage is a crime. Ladies, listen up: Those sensual, graceful proportions are a superwoman's ammunition.

And the best way to celebrate your womanhood is by indulging in your style options. Define your shape with a wide belt, try a floral print, wear siren red lipstick—maybe all at once. As women, we can completely alter our look from day to day. Ever wondered how you would be perceived as a blonde? Add some honey highlights or go platinum on a whim. Flirt with your own image by experimenting with stilettos or a lace camisole. Fabrics are another shortcut to accessing your femininity. I love silk charmeuse, chiffon, or lace on a woman because they add a flirty confection to a look.

Most importantly, tapping into your femininity will naturally encourage you to walk and stand and sit like a lady. Growing up in the South and studying ballet as a child, I was constantly reminded never to slouch or slump. "Imagine a broomstick at your back," my teachers would say. "Stand up straight. Sit up straight. Shoulders back." It may sound old-fashioned, but posture makes perfect. You can see the difference in the way your clothes bunch up and hang sadly if you hunch inward. Don't be a comma. You're an exclamation point. Throw back those shoulders and already you've completely altered your silhouette. Now just add high heels and cause a stir.

» And the best way to celebrate your womanhood is by indulging in all of your style options. Define your shape with a wide belt, try a floral print, wear siren red lipstick—maybe all at once.

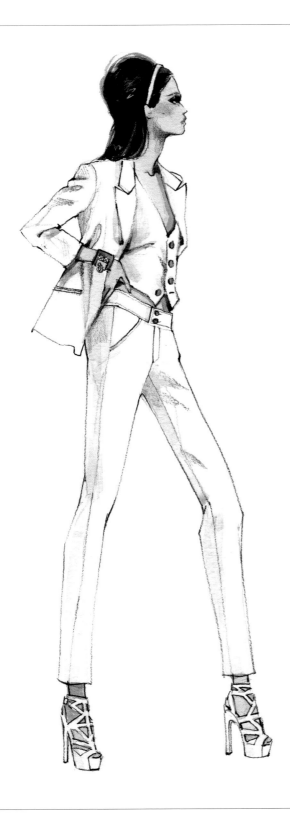

The art of androgyny

Dresses may be the obvious pinnacle of ladylike wear, but there's nothing more alluring—or feminine—than a woman who knows how to cross-dress. Menswear, with its structured lines, makes for the perfect contrast to a woman's natural curves. And it's a classic look that never dips out of style. Think of Katharine Hepburn in wide-leg trousers, tailored shirt, and a hacking jacket tossing her long auburn waves. Or sultry Marlene Dietrich, who smartly paired a fitted blazer with a lace blouse and inch-long false eyelashes. That juxtaposition of the femme and the fella is always a visual knockout.

In a three-piece suit, it's important to have the elements tailored to fit your body. I love a snug vest that shows off the female anatomy and even a peek of décolletage to drive home the "He's a she!" point. If you're daunted by the idea of head-to-toe haberdashery, you can wear just one masculine separate like a great double-breasted blazer. Or try a pair of high-heeled oxfords with slim cigarette pants or leggings.

» *When I costume ultra-ladylike Betty Draper in a tweed riding jacket and a silk ascot for an equestrian outing, the result is gender-bender brilliance.*

This is one ensemble that perfectly marries the masculine and the feminine. A tailored tuxedo jacket looks unbearably chic dressed up or dressed down.

When I costume ultra-ladylike Betty Draper in a tweed riding jacket and a silk ascot for an equestrian outing, the result is gender-bender brilliance. You can easily mimic the look by pairing knee boots with skinny jeans—tucked in, of course—and a blazer. Do add your Hermès scarf or a festive silk look-alike. If you're lean, you can even raid the boys' department of Brooks Brothers for a schoolboy blazer with engraved gold buttons.

Don't forgo those accessories, either. I'm a sucker for a lady in a derby or a fedora. A skinny woven or knit tie with a button-down works, too. Or you can play with a wide tie and a T-shirt and vest. Bow ties can be cute, but they are tougher to pull off. My all-time favorite use for a men's tie is to wear it as a belt à la Gene Kelly in *Singin' in the Rain*. Browse the men's department for inspiration or filch a few accents from your beau's stash. At a vintage or thrift shop, be on the lookout for a men's tuxedo shirt. Add some dazzle with the glint of gold or silver cuff links or a silk pocket square. Ladies: The sky is the limit, short of a mustache. (Look to Chapter 6 for more tips on accessories.)

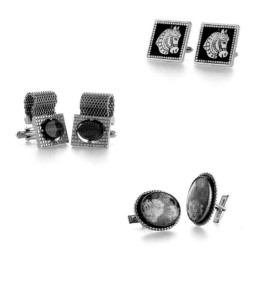

Chic cuff links from all different eras.

A nifty wool "cricket hat" by Tracy Watts.

My icons & inspirations

All this talk of leading ladies brings to mind a few of my favorite mesmerizing actresses. When I'm seeking motivation for a look or some new style cues, I often search for sirens who always made a grand entrance.

Clara Bow "the it girl"

THE
Onscreen Appeal

This 1920s silent screen star was literally the very first "it" girl and became one of the inspirations for Betty Boop. Would you expect any less from an actress who headlined movies like *Mantrap, Dangerous Curves,* and *Call Her Savage*? Bow's penchant for wearing siren red lipstick in an exaggerated heart shape spawned a trend, but I adore the dark-eyed minx for her wild, uproarious hair. Each titian curl was as rebellious as a suburban teenager. (When her fans learned that she used henna, the sales of the natural dye tripled.) She also shared my passion for exotic trims like furs and feathers. Just try ignoring a woman who makes an entrance in a halo of marabou.

THE
Offscreen Lesson

With no words to express herself, Bow relied on eye-rolling, saucy glances and those crazy curls to communicate. Obviously, she had to overdo it. But don't ever underestimate the power of body language. A sexy wink with the dip of a shoulder always trumps a "Nice to meet you." Practice a few of Bow's signature moves, like batting those lashes or widening those eyes, in the mirror. If your hair has a mind of its own, put aside the flat iron and bypass those styling products. Bow's wild mane became one of her most sexy attributes.

Louise Brooks
"the lustrous vamp"

THE
Onscreen Appeal

Once a chorus girl, this enchantress of the flapper era knew exactly how to draw attention to her brooding, gamine face with the right coif. Her storied bob, with its razor-straight bangs and pointed ends, announced her features as dramatically as a gilt picture frame. She often favored an ultralong strand of lustrous pearls à la Coco Chanel, which contrasted well with her dark hair and eyes. I always think of that famous 1928 Eugene Robert Richee photo of her in a black dress with the signature pearls encircling her silhouette.

THE
Offscreen Lesson

Brooks understood loyalty. If you find a look, be it a unique hairstyle or accessory, that sums up your persona in some way, marry it. Edith Head sported her sunglasses indoors long before Anna Wintour adopted the habit. Once Marilyn Monroe discovered that her mole accentuated her full lips, she never covered it up again. Talk to your hairdresser about cultivating a signature style with you. Or experiment with unexpected accessories like a men's pocket watch on a chain or a distinctive cocktail ring.

Jean Harlow
"the blonde bombshell"

THE
Onscreen Appeal

Known as the "blonde bombshell" for her platinum locks, Harlow never met a body-skimming, bias-cut dress she didn't like. The shinier the better. Watch her sidle onscreen in *Dinner at Eight*; she practically refracts light. I think of her as the pure female, a celebration of curves, and I consider Joan Holloway to be cut from the same luminous cloth. Both of these dames could hold their own, wisecracking with a mob of men. And how can you not adore a woman like Harlow, who chose to be buried in lingerie?

THE
Offscreen Lesson

Take a cue from this vixen and try a fabric like silk charmeuse or silk jersey, which fits the body like a coat of latex paint. (Shapewear is highly recommended.) Harlow was also renowned for her brassy blend of grit and wit. Meaning it's more than okay to be tough and self-possessed. Telling a racy joke or two never hurts, either.

THE
Onscreen Appeal

Hayworth changed her hair color eight times for different movies during her career, but her radiance never faltered. Just watch *Gilda* (1946) and take notes during that legendary scene where she shimmies and sings "Put the Blame on Mame." Her strapless black satin dress designed by Columbia Pictures costume designer Jean Louis has inspired countless red carpet copies. Hayworth, whose heritage was a blend of Spanish, Irish, and English, once said, "I think all women have a certain elegance about them which is destroyed when they take off their clothes." Notice how seductively she peels off one opera-length black glove in that same scene? Now that's a real striptease.

Rita Hayworth
"the glamour-puss"

THE
Offscreen Lesson

Every woman should own one knockout dress. It may be strapless, snug, and satin or a delicately printed sheath. This is the dress that makes you feel smarter, sexier, and skinnier as soon as you slip it over your head. Call it your "Gilda" dress and just be sure you can shimmy in it.

THE
Onscreen Appeal

Where to begin? Those violet eyes, with their upward tilt, couldn't be more captivating. Never mind that head of shiny raven curls and matching fringe of black lashes. When I watch Taylor's films, I am always intrigued by her silky diction and her ability to glide so gracefully into a scene like a panther. But it's the white, sleeveless chiffon dress in *Cat on a Hot Tin Roof,* designed by Helen Rose, that always makes me press Pause and sigh. The full, accordion pleated skirt and fitted waist couldn't be more flattering to her figure.

Elizabeth Taylor
"the queen of sultry"

THE
Offscreen Lesson

Contrast, contrast, contrast. That collision of different shades or shapes can make a look scream "Wow" rather than whisper. Taylor wore white because it absolutely opposed her ebony hair and deep purple eyes. In fact, white is one of my favorite shades because it reflects light and adds a youthful buoyancy. If you think you can only wear white to your own wedding, it's time to revisit it.

Brigitte Bardot
"the bohemian beauty"

THE
Onscreen Appeal

Effortless beauty. That's what comes to mind whenever I see pictures of this stunning French sexpot, whether she's wearing a bikini or a bath towel or a belted leotard. It's been said that a postcard picture of her in just a white corset outsold souvenir postcards of the Eiffel Tower in Paris back in 1960. Her tousled hair only adds to that "Who, *moi?*" careless look. Somehow, Bardot always manages to appear as if she spent only thirty seconds getting ready and yet she still looks like a million bucks.

THE
Offscreen Lesson

Ever belabored every aspect of an outfit? Maybe you forever fussed over the knot of a silk scarf after subjecting your hair to a take-no-prisoners blowout. Or you tried on every single pair of shoes until you found the gray suede pump that best matches the pinstripe in a suit. Bardot would have already polished off a bottle of Beaujolais in the amount of time it took you to get ready. If you want to be less studied about your appearance, shake out your mane and wear a pair of sandals that don't match your belt. Or mix patterns like stripes and florals. Pretend that your style is on spring break—in Saint-Tropez, of course.

Dressing up, when dressing down

Some people shudder at the idea of getting dressed up. Not me. I would wear a ball gown every single day of my life if I could— look out Scarlett O'Hara. (As a little girl I was known for changing complete outfits three or four times in a day! Tights and shoes included.) Of course, there's a time— preferably after sunset—and place for a strapless column gown with a mermaid train. But the concept of dressing up shouldn't be reserved for weddings and black-tie occasions. You can always add polish to any look, be it casual or cocktail attire.

Thankfully, the style aesthetic of *Mad Men* rivals my own passion for looking sharp. And I'm thrilled that the look of the show has ushered in a new appreciation for getting decked out. People always tell me I inspire them to go that extra mile with their outfits, not to mention to order a martini. To me, that's an amazing compliment because I know that the energy spent always pays off tenfold. You not only feel great and present a better self when you dress up, but you also prompt others to match your efforts.

Every day, take a little extra time to finesse your look. Even just five minutes. Think of it as simply seasoning your signature dish. It's an easy exercise and you'll quickly adopt the habit of naturally honing your personal style.

Here are ten style shortcuts for taking a look to the next level. Each one of these upgrades works for day or night and instantly makes you look like you put some extra effort into your appearance.

» Every day, take a little extra time to finesse your look. Even just five minutes. Think of it as simply seasoning your signature dish. It's an easy exercise and you'll quickly adopt the habit of naturally honing your personal style.

Here are ten style shortcuts for taking a look to the next level.

Go animal.
Faux fur or feather are the fast lane to drama. Try an ostrich-feather or marabou collar to make a splash with any look. Zebra- and leopard-print accents like shoes or belts have a similar primal effect.

Use your head.
Hair can make or break an outfit. A modern updo always lends sophistication to any attire. For a more casual finish, you could opt for a sleek blowout.

Heighten the drama.
High heels add polish to any look and add oomph to any silhouette. (Even my flats have two-inch heels.) Try stilettos, wedges, or platforms.

Grab a bag.

Purses are the ultimate arm trophies. When going that extra yard, carry one that stands out because of its unique shape, design, or color.

See red.

The perfect crimson lipstick or sexy smoky eye can be more powerful than a police siren. Be sure to accentuate one facial feature when dressing up. (See a detailed how-to on makeup in Chapter 6 starting on page 129.)

Top it off.

A simple pair of jeans gets a major jump-start with a high-octane jacket with ornamental buttons or hardware. Vivid prints like plaid and heady fabrics like brocade create the same result.

Glam up the gams.

Lace or patterned stockings will enliven any little black dress. Experiment with fishnets (black or nude) or small-polka-dotted hosiery. Colored tights add flair; dark colors like black, plum, or slate gray are the easiest to wear.

Go chapeau.
Thankfully, hats are making a major comeback. Adorn your head with a jaunty cocktail hat or an elaborately feathered headband and you're suddenly the conversation piece.

Arm yourself.
A great modern pair of gloves harkens back to better-dressed decades. For a formal evening affair, go with opera length. A pair of two-tone driving gloves adds flash to a more casual getup.

Adorn accordingly.
Cuffs, layered chains, cocktail rings, and chandelier earrings are all bold pieces that announce an arrival.

Cocktail
CHATTER

THE FAMED COSTUME DESIGNER ADRIAN—ADRIAN ADOLPH GREENBERG—worked with Hollywood's most elegant leading ladies, including Jean Harlow, Katharine Hepburn, and Joan Crawford. The deliciously flamboyant designs seen in the fashion show scene of 1939's *The Women* showcase his range. But it was his ferocious loyalty to glamour that makes him such a legend. He once said, "It was because of Garbo that I left MGM. In her last picture they wanted to make her a sweater girl, a real American type. I said, 'When the glamour ends for Garbo, it also ends for me.'"

A FEMME FATALE, which translates to "deadly woman" in French, uses her feminine wiles to bewitch a man and lead him far astray. I love the seemingly innocent look of silent-screen vamp Theda Bara, who pioneered the way for future cinematic *femmes fatales* like Barbara Stanwyck and Lana Turner.

WOMEN AND TROUSERS GO WAY BACK, ACTUALLY. Persian ladies donned pants as early as the fourth century, but Westerners didn't dabble in menswear until the Victorian period. In the early 1850s, Amelia Jenks Bloomer popularized baggy pants cuffed at the ankle to be worn beneath shorter skirts. But men scoffed and "bloomers" hardly became all the rage.

CHECKLIST

Discover and hone your signature style—whether it's a preference for bright floral patterns or bold accessories.

Try on pieces in three colors you have never worn before next time you visit a boutique. Hold each shade next to your face to see if brightens your complexion or intensifies your eye color.

En route to the kitchen, practice walking like a lady with your spine straight and shoulders thrown back. Extra points for doing so in high heels.

Experiment with one menswear-inspired separate like a vest, fedora, or schoolboy blazer.

Take a style cue from Brigitte Bardot and let loose your inner-boho goddess with a tousled high ponytail or a leotard paired with a peasant skirt.

DEFINING your SILHOUETTE
AND SECRETS FOR DRESSING YOUR SHAPE

2

If only we could all be backlit every morning as we dressed for the day. That may sound a bit alarming, but then you would see the true shape that your undergarments and clothes create on your body. And that outline, with its glorious curves and slopes and dips, is your all-important silhouette. Consider it your style calling card.

The word itself actually hails from the name of an eighteenth-century French finance minister, Étienne de Silhouette, who loved to snip paper portraits. Later, with the invention of crinoline steel and preposterous fashion proportions, *silhouette* came to describe the human form. In fact, I love fashion because it's all about that manipulation of the human form, and different periods accentuate different parts of the body.

Take the 1870s, when the bustle emerged. This exaggeration of the backside was a reaction to the hoop skirt, which had transformed women into giant bells. Twenty years later, the leg-of-mutton period focused on women's upper half, and puffy sleeves and pigeon fronts injected volume up top. Flash forward to the roaring 1920s and corsetry disappears, so women in drop-waisted flapper dresses appear as linear as planks of wood. Hemlines shortened in the forties during wartime because of a shortage of fabric and then extended in the 1950s, when excess was celebrated in long, full poodle skirts.

The silhouettes you see on *Mad Men*, which takes place during the early 1960s, are so flattering because that era stole inspiration from architecture and sculpture. Hemlines crept up from the mid-calf to just below or above the knee, so you glimpse those shapely legs. Come 1964, the miniskirt hits the scene and steals the show. The outlines then relax in the 1970s and gypsy-style skirts and peasant blouses reinvent the form as liquid. And who can forget the eighties? Shoulder pads and leggings gave us all superwomen silhouettes.

Finding the style and cut of clothes that suit you best comes from experimentation and knowing your body type. If you're curvy on top and bottom, achieving that late-fifties bombshell form—a favorite of Joan Holloway—should be your aim. More athletic and slim? Dabble in the flapper look of the twenties. Even better, you can flirt with all different silhouettes just by changing your outfits. Come. The mirror beckons.

» Hemlines shortened in the forties during wartime because of a shortage of fabric and then extended in the 1950s, when excess was celebrated in long, full poodle skirts.

» *Who can forget the eighties?*
Shoulder pads and leggings gave
us all superwomen silhouettes.

*Joan's vintage 1960s hot pink boiled wool sheath—
worn in season two—complements both her sensual
curves and her fair complexion.*

Only self-appreciation allowed

When actors come into my fitting room, it's very important that they don't self-criticize. It's a social symptom of this epidemic of insecurity and body distortion. And we all indulge in this habit of scolding ourselves for not being perfect in our own eyes. Society even condones it. For that reason, I strictly enforce a feel-good rule that everyone must obey: Only self-appreciation is allowed in the fitting room. Praise your curves and give thanks for those fantastic legs.

As a costume designer, my ultimate goal is to make sure that my actresses find their characters. But it's equally important to me that they feel absolutely beautiful along the way. After all, these women spend a lot of time staring into a huge mirror as their costumes are being fitted. That crucial

my eyes," or "This dress will look fantastic on me." It may sound silly at first. (You can whisper it, if you must.) But eventually you'll notice that your forced optimism has transformed into a natural enthusiasm for getting ready.

» *Only self-appreciation is allowed in the fitting room. Praise your curves and give thanks for those fantastic legs.*

transformation can take place only if an actor feels great about her appearance.

Apply the same rule to your own personal fitting room, whether it be your closet or bedroom. Before you get dressed, hold up your outfit and admire the color or cut of the collar. Take a moment to appreciate the fabric and say something positive aloud like, "I just know this blouse is going to bring out

The new-you resolution

At the end of every year, most of us vow to jettison our vices and to shed a few pounds. But what if you resolved instead to change the way you view your body? Rather than bemoaning your backside or cursing your calves, you could appraise your figure from a different, kinder perspective and come to appreciate—and even celebrate—every curve.

Not so long ago, I made it my goal to become my own best ally. (Keep in mind that as a costume designer, I am never without a trusty tape measure. That can be dangerous.) My personal foe at the time was what I conceived to be my not-so-slender ankles, and my glare went directly to them whenever I got dressed. No matter the outfit, my ankles interfered. They sullied my self-esteem. Clearly, it was time to stifle my inner critic.

One morning I stripped down in front of my mirror and had an epiphany. Instead of denouncing a mole or a wrinkle or my ankles, I decided that I would embrace every single aspect of my body. You can do this, too, by taking ten minutes in the morning to scan yourself—from head to toe—and then praise every last feature. If you find yourself nit-picking about a few wrinkles, stop and stare at them in a new light. Those lines not only add character, they also proclaim a life filled with experiences and laughs. The same goes for freckles, which add a sprinkling of your European heritage.

Do this exercise every day for a month and you'll discover that you have rebooted your brain's tendency to self-negate by reinforcing a new behavior. According to neuropsychology it takes about four to six weeks to break bad habits by changing our neural patterns. The benefits are endless. Not only will your confidence buoy, but you'll carry yourself taller and project a more positive self-image. You might even come to love your mirror.

Spotlight a great asset

Now that you're over the moon for your anatomy, it's time to play favorites. Take a moment to consider your best asset. It could be any part of your body, from your smile to your clavicle to your ankles. If you can't decide on one asset simply because you adore every inch of yourself, bravo. You can accentuate a different one every day of the week.

More likely, however, you're squinting down at your hips in the mirror at this very moment and shaking your head. Remember my rule: Only positive thoughts while you're in any state of nakedness. You may want to focus in on whichever feature lassos the most compliments. Once you have isolated your sweet spot, it's time to shine a spotlight on it. Here are some stylish ways for accentuating each asset:

Face: Any open neckline—from a V-style to a portrait to a scoop—is almost like an arrow pointing up. It draws the eyes directly to your visage. (A bold necklace will steal the gaze.) A pair of bejeweled earrings also brings attention to your eyes and smile.

Long neck: Hair worn up—in a high ponytail or a chic bun—allows for full view of a long neck. Audrey Hepburn opted for a pixie cut so her slender swan neck would never compete with her hair. Dangling chandelier earrings, too, extend that line from the chin to the shoulders. Opt for a metal or stones that contrast with your hair color.

Shoulders: Bare shoulders are unbelievably sexy, so do show them off in dresses and tops with halters, spaghetti straps, or no straps at all. Grecian-style gowns or a sweetheart neckline will do the trick, too.

Bust: There's nothing sexier than an open neckline. Choose sweetheart, V-neck, or scoop styles that offer a glimpse of décolletage. And a great-fitting bra is an absolute must. (Refer to the primer on bra fitting on page 40.)

Waist: One word: cinch. The svelte waist can be exaggerated with a skinny or wide belt clasped at the narrowest point. Add a full skirt and the waist appears even smaller, which highlights upper and lower curves. Pick out garments that include a waist seam and, hence, nip in the center.

Derrière: A tailored pencil skirt is your secret weapon. You can also accent your lower half with white jeans or lighter-toned fabrics. Short jackets that skim the waist will also attract the eye to your backside.

Legs: Lucky you. Minidresses, spandex, or knit leggings, cigarette pants, and short, pleated skirts are all welcome in your closet. You can also show them off with skinny or stovepipe jeans.

I love the color play of the amethyst and garnet crystals on these chandelier earrings.

Know thy measurements

You can conveniently forget your age, but you had better be clear on your bust size. Almost 80 percent of women don't know if they're a 36B or a 38C. Even a half-inch can make a huge difference in the fit and visual effect of a bra. On *Mad Men*, all the leading ladies know the importance of great undergarments. That's because I measure every actress for her precise bust, waist, and hip stats. It's the only way I can be sure that every garment is cut to fit just right.

You should do the same. Knowing your measurements is especially key when you're shopping for vintage, since labels often don't carry sizes. (Also, vintage sizes run anywhere from 2 to 6 sizes smaller than today's sizing system. If you're a 6, you may wear a 10 or 12 in a 1950s cocktail dress.) You can gauge an outfit's width and length with a tape measure, which is how I find some of my favorite looks for *Mad Men*.

Here's how to get your most accurate measurements:

Bust: Loop the tape measure around your back and across the center of your breasts. Be sure to lay the tape flat, but don't cinch.

» *Almost 80 percent of women don't know if they're a 36B or a 38C. Even a half-inch can make a huge difference in the fit and visual effect of a bra.*

Waist: You can find your natural waist with your hands by placing them on the narrowest point of the abdomen. (Your ribs are above your hands and your hips are below.) Now use the tape to measure around that narrow point.

Hips: To find your hip size, measure to exactly seven inches below your waist. Don't forget to go around your buttocks and, again, no cinching.

The foundations: *bras to girdles to garters*

Your silhouette starts with your foundation garments. The right bra can cantilever your bust to create the perfect perky contour or a hint of cleavage. A girdle or body shaper will smooth away any overspill and broaden your style options to include dress cuts and fabrics that you may have ruled out in the past. For *Mad Men* fittings, I have an arsenal of undergarments that includes long-line bras, garters, merry widow corsets, and boned girdles that physically prod you to stand up straighter.

How do you think Joan Holloway achieves that seamless hourglass silhouette with nary a visual hiccup to her sensuous curves? She wears a long-line bra that comes down to her waist and a closed-bottom girdle, which resembles a pair of modern-day bicycle shorts, with boning and garters. Yes, they can be a tad uncomfortable. In fact, all the leading ladies of *Mad Men* had some issues with their restrictive lingerie at first. But as seasons passed, they fell in love with their undergarments because they helped them to inhabit their characters. "I love my bra. I love my girdle," Christina Hendricks now announces when she comes into my fitting room.

To find the right undergarments, you first need to determine your desired silhouette. Modern shapewear like Spanx's Slim Cognito (a high-waisted, mid-thigh body suit) or Maidenform's Control It! High-Waist Thigh-Slimmer that extends to

» *The right bra can cantilever your bust to create the perfect perky contour or a hint of cleavage.*

A seemingly demure but truly sexy Edgy Girl balconette bra by Felina.

the knee is also essential. You want the upper and lower foundations to meet to ensure that flawless outline. For Betty's ultra nipped waist, I outfit her in a strapless and boned merry widow corset, which further tapers the midsection to its most narrow point. I think you get the best fit when you work with a lingerie salesperson, who can verify your measurements and suggest specific styles.

Practicality aside, great lingerie makes you feel polished and feminine—even if no one else gets a glimpse. Joan's wardrobe also calls for dainty slips in hot pink, royal blue, and black lace that match her dresses. Betty always wears white underpinnings, which suit her persona as the perpetual perfect bride. Don't wait for a special occasion like your wedding or a romantic getaway to update your bras and panties and invest in a few provocative pieces. Collect them for yourself.

Vintage Maidenform ads.

» *A girdle or body shaper will smooth away any overspill and broaden your style options to include dress cuts and fabrics that you may have ruled out in the past.*

Felina's flirty, padded Uptown Girl bra with matching ruffled skirt.

Three bras every woman should own

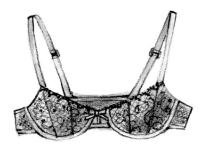

Balconette bra: This Jezebel underwire style modeled after the demi bra works overtime by uplifting and slightly compressing the bust to create a shelf of cleavage. The cut makes it perfect for plunging or open necklines.

» This underwire style modeled after the demi bra works overtime by uplifting and slightly compressing the bust to create a shelf of cleavage.

T-shirt bra: This seamless style is usually made of microfiber and won't be visible beneath clingy fabrics like cotton tees and ultralight knits. If you're looking to enhance your bust, try Maidenform's new Ultimate Push Up Bra, which makes you two cup sizes bigger.

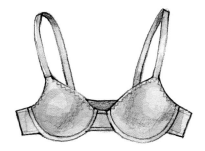

Strapless bra: Essential for wearing Grecian gowns, strap-free and skinny-strap styles, halter tops, and tanks. Try one from Elle Macpherson. Note: Buy it one cup size smaller than your typical bra fit to ensure that it stays put and provides proper support.

HOW TO ACHIEVE BRA BLISS

An improperly fitted bra doesn't do justice to your assets or flatter your natural silhouette. Karen Valenti, a fit specialist with Maidenform, conducts in-store bra clinics to ensure that women understand their measurements. (A salesperson should be able to fit you for a bra at most department stores.) She suggests that you recheck measurements after gaining or losing five or more pounds or having a baby. "Most women are wearing bras that are too small," she says. "Or they don't realize that their size might vary, from style to style."

How to measure yourself

Band Measurement Most women measure their rib cage under their breasts to get their band measurement. To double-check the measurement, wrap a tape measure snugly around your back, under your arms, and across the top of your chest. This is another technique to assess your band size. Keep in mind your rib cage expands and contracts when you breathe, so by taking both measurements you'll get the best indication of your band size for a more comfortable fit.

Cup Measurement With your bra on, wrap a measuring tape around your back and across the fullest part of your bust, and take a gentle measurement. To get your cup size, subtract your band measurement from this measurement. If the difference is . . .

Courtesy of Maidenform

1" = A CUP	3" = C CUP	5" = DD CUP
2" = B CUP	4" = D CUP	6" = DDD CUP

Example:

Cup measurement = 39   Band measurement = 36

3-inch difference = size 36C

The right fit

Your silhouette rides on the fit. If the fabric pulls at the pockets or puckers at the waist, you lose that clean line. Knowing your measurements and your body type will help guide you in choosing cuts and styles that complement your natural shape. But be sure to test-drive every outfit while you pose in front of the mirror. Can you walk comfortably? Does sitting cause the fabric to bunch or stretch too much? (I wish all stores had a chair in the dressing room so you could perch for a moment before the mirror.) Take in the marvelous view from all angles: front, back, and profile.

Certain great pieces may require a tuck in the waist or a new hem, and you shouldn't bypass them for that reason. On *Mad Men*, my cutter-fitter Joanna Bradley, who has worked with me ever since I designed for HBO's *Deadwood*, knows the figures and little anatomical nuances of every actor on the show. Most dry cleaners employ a tailor who can handle simple alterations for less than ten dollars. If you're willing to devote more time and a bit more money to fit—which I do recommend—you can work with someone regularly who will record all of your "tailor measurements," from cuffs to inseams. Talk to him or her about the assets you always want to enhance and any areas you would prefer to minimize. Ask for input. I like to think of tailors as magicians who can make things like love handles disappear. But before you hand over that ultra-expensive designer dress or jacket for reworking, have your tailor perform a simple hem on dress pants so you can gauge the workmanship.

Everybody, every body: *the four basic body types*

Costume designers dress the world. I like to say that I design for everyone, from a size 2 to a size 22 and anything in between. A script could call for all types, ranging from rambunctious tots to sexy secretaries to demure housewives to chic mistresses. My tape measure never discriminates.

On *Mad Men*, in particular, I create looks for every shape, size, and age. Obviously, petite Betty Draper couldn't borrow one of voluptuous Joan Holloway's pencil skirts. Nor would broad-shouldered Don Draper swap jackets with flinty Pete Campbell. For me, it's exciting to dress all these different physiques. Not to mention the fact that I am thrilled to see how the look of *Mad Men* has empowered so many women to rejoice in their curves and femininity.

In order to accentuate those awesome contours, you must first familiarize yourself with your core shape. As they say, knowledge is power. Once you understand your natural silhouette, it's easy enough to enhance assets or make some nips and tucks with the right wardrobe.

THE
Delicious Apple

A woman who is an apple carries most of her weight in her midsection. This imbalance can make you look shorter and wider if you don't counteract the proportions. *Objective:* To minimize the midsection and draw all eyes to those great, thin legs.

Wardrobe staples:
- Cute A-line shifts, short skirts, blouses with a gently curved waistline.
- Single-button jackets, wrap shirts and dresses, pants that flare at the leg or wide-legged trousers.
- Long fitted shirts and sweaters that fall to the hips also disguise a full midriff.

Indulge:
- Long necklaces and pearls that draw the eye downward.
- Fine knits like cashmere.
- Bohemian tunics.
- You can also experiment with bold-colored bottoms like colored denim or skirts with geometric or floral prints.

Avoid:
- Bold patterns such as stripes on tops.
- Shiny fabrics like satins.
- Short jackets and sweaters that skim the waist.
- Tapered pants like capris or skinny jeans.
- Shoulder pads so you don't exaggerate the disparity of proportions.
- Chunky knits.

Optimum neckline: A cowl neck, scoop, or V-neck creates the illusion of an elongated torso.

Your best-cut dress: An empire cut waist that falls just below the bust with an A-line or flared skirt.

Jeans of choice: A trouser cut with a higher waistband and a simple straight leg. Step away from anything with a low rise.

Your ideal bathing suit: A one-piece with a plunging neckline will help to define a waist. In a bikini, look for solid halter tops and printed bottoms. Ruffles, bows, or ties on bikini bottoms will also add balance.

<u>THE</u>
Succulent Pear

Just as it sounds, a woman with a pear-shape body stores most of her weight below the waistline. Fuller hips and thighs contrast with narrow shoulders, a smaller bust, and a slim midriff. *Objective:* To detract from the hips, which are the widest points of your silhouette, and focus on arms and shoulders.

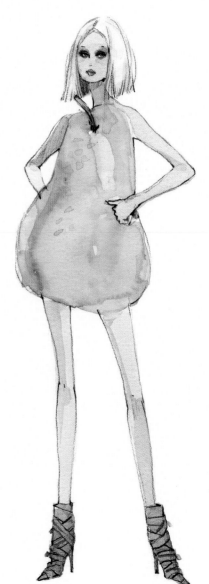

Wardrobe staples:
• A-line or full skirts, brightly colored button-down shirts and patterned blouses, jackets that skim the waist or mid-thigh.
• Flat-front pants with a wide leg that skim the hips will make you look taller.

Indulge:
• Turtlenecks.
• Blazers.
• Wide-collared shirts or ones with draping or ruching or puffed sleeves that add balance to your proportions.

Avoid:
• Cargo pants or bottoms with lots of pocket detail.
• Patterned or light-colored pants.
• Straight skirts and bias-cut dresses.

Optimum neckline: Intricate beading or detail work on a neckline draw the eye away from hips. Try a boat neck or go strapless for some upper wow.

Your best-cut dress: Sleeveless or spaghetti-strapped styles that flare to A-line or full skirts are swell because they accentuate your upper half.

Denim of choice: Mid-rise waistbands and wide legs to accommodate thighs or flared legs like a boot-cut work best. Bigger pockets will appear to minimize the backside.

Your ideal bathing suit: A high-cut bottom elongates the legs, and opt for a darker shade. On top, go with embellishments like ruffles or ruching or bold prints and bright colors. In a one-piece, look for padded cups to enhance the bust.

THE
Slim Ruler

The woman with an athletic, lean build has fewer curves and more of a straight up-and-down figure. But, in fact, you share your shape with runway models and can wear almost anything. *Objective:* To create some contours and add femininity to the silhouette by accentuating the waist.

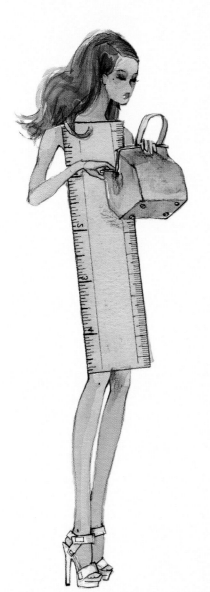

Wardrobe staples:
• Bias-cut jackets or flare-cut and pencil skirts add curves. Trapeze dresses and slim-cut pants and trousers work, too.
• Baby-doll and pussy-bow blouses inject girlishness, while wide and skinny belts and vests define the waist.

Indulge:
• Pieces with ladylike accents like ruffles, pleats, and peplum.
• Florals and graphic prints also add some depth to the silhouette.
• Jackets with darts at the waist and wide lapels lend curvature.

Avoid:
• Bolero jackets and short-waisted tops bisect the figure and minimize curves.
• Vertical lines can accentuate the ruler shape.

Optimum neckline: Wrap tops, scoops, or V-necks emphasize the bust and draw the eye to the face. A padded bra with underwire will help add contours.

Your best-cut dress: Halter tops with full skirts and any style frocks with a V-neck and a drop waist.

Jeans of choice: Low-rise jeans with detailed or embellished pockets add some definition to your backside. But all styles, from skinny jeans to high-waisted trousers, work for you.

Your ideal bathing suit: String bikinis or lightly padded demi-cut tops with an underwire enhance the bust. Ruffles, ruching, and embellishments add some pop to the bustline, too. A color-blocked tankini helps define a waist.

THE
Curvy Hourglass

You have deliciously symmetrical curves, with an exaggerated bust and hip line. That narrow waist only heightens the va-va-voom silhouette. *Objective:* Show off that waist, which will become the sexy focal point of your silhouette.

Wardrobe staples:
· A bra with amazing support! Wrap tops and blouses that nip at the waist.
· Flat-front, side-zip, and pocketless pants—preferably with boot-cut or flared bottoms.

Indulge:
· High-waisted slacks.
· Light-knit cardigans.
· Belted jackets or coats.

Avoid:
· Shifts or trapeze dresses that hide your shape.
· Any styles that overemphasize the hips, like a gathered skirt.

Optimum neckline: V-neck, portrait, sweetheart, and off-the-shoulder styles flatter.

Your best-cut dress: One word: sheath. Wrap dresses in jersey or light cotton and styles with princess-seamed bodices also work well.

Jeans of choice: A higher rise will solve gaping at the waistband, and seek out jeans with flare at the leg and some stretch (Lycra) to let curves breathe.

Your ideal bathing suit: A halter-top style or bandeau with high-waisted bottom is a great retro style that works.

Cocktail CHATTER

ALL OF YOUR SUMS ADD UP TO A MUCH GREATER PART.
In the 1957 comedy *Love in the Afternoon*, Audrey Hepburn
exclaims: "I'm too thin and my ears stick out
and my teeth are crooked and my neck's too long."
Gary Cooper counters with: "Maybe. But I love the
way it all hangs together."

WHEN IT COMES TO INCHES, WHO'S COUNTING? The studio Twentieth Century Fox claimed that Marilyn Monroe was a 37-23-36, while her dressmaker recorded her measurements as 35-22-35. Either way, Monroe was a modern-day size 8 or 10.

IN THE 1940S, LOCKHEED DEEMED BRAS MANDATORY FOR THEIR FEMALE EMPLOYEES BECAUSE OF "GOOD TASTE, ANATOMICAL SUPPORT AND MORALE." That same decade, the torpedo or bullet bra, thought to be modeled after the nose of a military fighter plane, helped define busty actresses like Jane Russell as "sweater girls."

CHECKLIST

Stand in front of a full-length mirror and admire your assets aloud. For instance, say, "I love the contours of my hips" or "My bare shoulders are sensuous."

On your next shopping foray, try on two pieces that accentuate one of your favorite features. If you want to highlight your waistline, model a pencil skirt or a wide belt nipped at your most narrow point.

If you haven't already taken a measurement tape to your hips, waist, and bust, do so right now. Or solicit a salesperson's help. And commit those figures to memory!

Take stock of your undergarments and gradually build a wardrobe that includes shapewear like Spanx and three essential bras: the balconette, the strapless, and the T-shirt style.

Determine your basic body type, based on the four shapes described in the chapter, and check to see if your current separates and dresses flatter your frame.

The
DRESSING
ROOM

3

I learned long ago that a closet could be your ultimate ally or most insidious adversary. Who hasn't frantically foraged through a snake pit of belts to complete an outfit before running out the door? Or wrestled with a legion of empty dry-cleaning bags to get to a certain dress?

I finally resolved to banish that needless agony from my life by renaming my closet a "dressing room"—a more glamorous moniker—and employing my costume designer know-how for grouping and storing my belongings.

Mind you, I needed professional help to carry out my conviction. Because the walk-in space off my bedroom was long and narrow, built-ins had to be installed to optimize the floor-to-ceiling real estate. Shoes, forever an addiction, seemed to mate and disappear beneath racks, so a closet designer added a special shoe wardrobe. Now my pink satin Valentino sling-backs share a shelf with other favorite footwear like a pair of Brooks Brothers "Black Fleece" high-heeled, two-toned oxfords (see pages 50 and 51) and vintage Terry de Havilland sandals. Purses, too, have their own special nooks, so a 1940s crocheted clutch and an exquisite hand-painted silk frame bag from the fifties are easily accessible.

The number-one rule for creating a formidable dressing room is to make everything visible. Conceptualizing a fantastic outfit requires viewing an open landscape of possibilities. My collection of twenty or so formal gowns, maxi dresses, and the silk palazzo jumpsuit from the 1960s are catalogued on a rack that sits tall enough so that they don't graze the floor. The same principle applies for long coats, of course. If you don't have a high rack, you can store coats and long dresses in hanging garment bags that fold over. Your clothes must endure enough peril while being worn, so don't jeopardize their condition when they're not in use. I always hang up my tailored pieces and delicates to preserve the fabric and condition.

Vintage furs, including a beaver-fur collar with knife pleating from the 1890s and a scallop-edged muff, have their own special cabinet, too. Belts, including my 1980s hammered metal (a nod to Michael Jackson) and sequined ones, hang vertically from pegs so that I can quickly access that final accent. Full disclosure: I do have a drawer of rolled-up belts that need to be hung, as well. Hey, a dressing room is always a work in progress.

Once you have assessed the organizational needs of your dressing room, focus on the ambience. Consider your closet an extension of the bedroom or living room and decorate it with the very same panache. Paint the walls a light, bright color and add a stylish kilim or geometric-pattern area rug if the floors are hardwood. Add a few framed photos or objets d'art or even a bouquet of fresh flowers to the shelves. The full-length mirror must be as honest as your most tactless relative, so pick one that doesn't elongate your figure. (Such false flattery will only frustrate you when you later glimpse a more realistic reflection elsewhere.)

Lighting, too, should be your conspirator. Avoid fluorescent bulbs, which cast a greenish blue hue that doesn't humor your pallor or clothing colors. After all, who wants to look seasick? Incandescent bulbs impart a warm, yellowish glow that adds an aura of radiance. Trust me, creating an inviting environment in your dressing room will pay off every single morning.

Valentino pink silk
satin slingbacks.

Deliciously retro two-toned oxford pumps from Brooks Brothers' Black Fleece label.

SMALL CLOSET SOLUTIONS

If you're short on storage space, you need to be diligent about organization and pruning out pieces you no longer wear. Here are three quick tips for creating more square footage:

Archive by season.

Once winter passes, remove those heavy woolens, bulky sweaters, and coats from your inventory and pack them in vacuum storage bags or plastic cubes. Limiting your selection to seasonally appropriate clothes opens up plenty of space.

Sleep on it. Create more

room by storing certain special occasion pieces and accessories in under-the-bed storage chests and shoe organizers.

Label like a neat freak.

If you're short on racks and shelves, you may have to store pieces in cubes or bins. Be sure to classify all items, from sandals to scarves, with labels to make foraging quick and easy.

Adult dress-up

Remember that unmistakable kick of playing dress-up as a little girl? You would fling open the doors to your mother's closet and gape at the dizzying possibilities. Perhaps red shoes with skyscraper heels or dresses edged in exotic lace and satin slips awaited. Within moments you had ransacked her wardrobe and teetered to the mirror.

Nowadays I prefer to loot my own closet. Playing dress-up actually relaxes and inspires me because I appreciate the variety of my clothes, especially when I throw together inconceivable outfits that you would only wear to a costume ball. Seriously, though, it's the perfect way to experiment with new combinations without feeling harried about getting ready or running late. It also enables you to take stock of your inventory and even happen upon a forgotten piece like a slinky silk tank or a chiffon wrap trimmed with ostrich feathers. Plus you can test-drive an outfit around the house so that you feel more comfortable when you wear it out for the first time.

Of course, dress-up should always be an adventure. It helps to pretend that you're seeing everything in your closet for the first time. That way you can appraise your inventory with a fresh perspective and even take a moment to admire your own taste and sense of style. By all means, do pat yourself on the back for buying that tulip skirt on sale or splurging on the beaded bolero jacket.

Like any game, this version of dress-up does have a few rules:

Put together surprising, new ensembles you have never tried before. For instance, pair a romantic, floral blouse with a leather miniskirt or add a long cardigan to a maxi dress. Even what feels like a kooky combination could pay off. Be bold.

Take a plunge with accessories. Layer strands of pearls, belt a scarf or long chain with a flashy pendant, or try a brooch as a hair clip. For extra points, do all three at once and maybe you'll be thrilled with the dramatic outcome.

Experiment with past seasons' items you have neglected. You can refresh last season's bubble skirt with a pair of platform ankle boots or add some verve to a vintage khaki trench coat with a bright red belt.

Set aside pieces that need to be ironed or repaired. Dress-up is a delicious way to tackle some spring cleaning and prepare your closet for those mornings you oversleep and have just five minutes to get ready and look fantastic.

Be a supermodel in front of the mirror and do your best catwalk moves. Thrust your right hip forward, throw those shoulders back, and pout. It's always good practice for making your next look-at-me entrance.

*THIS PAGE: Two pearl and
rhinestone necklaces by Carolee.*

*OPPOSITE: A darling 1960s
heart-shaped brooch.*

» *Layer strands of pearls, belt a scarf or long chain with a flashy
pendant, or try a brooch as a hair clip. For extra points, do all three
at once and maybe you'll be thrilled with the dramatic outcome.*

My favorite accessories

Here are a few of my most prized accessories, gleaned from my ever-expanding collection. Sometimes, a little accent goes a long way.

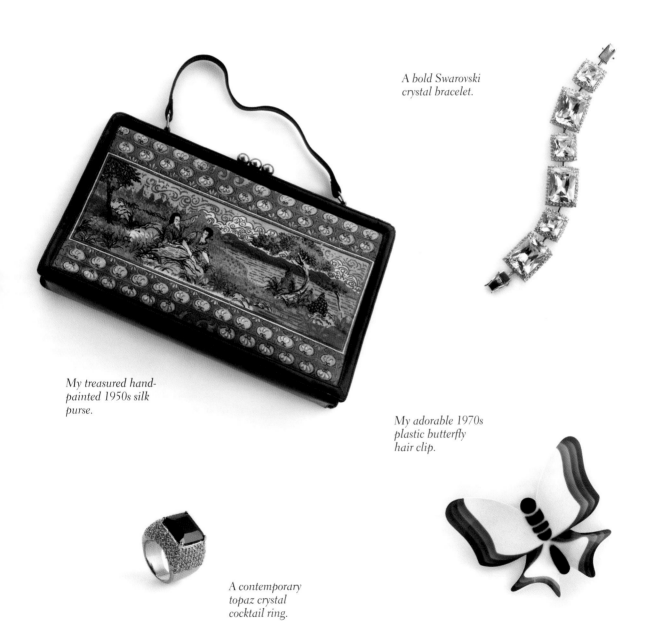

A bold Swarovski crystal bracelet.

My treasured hand-painted 1950s silk purse.

My adorable 1970s plastic butterfly hair clip.

A contemporary topaz crystal cocktail ring.

*My grandmother's glitzy
rhinestone shoe clips.*

*Replica 1860
drop earrings.*

*A statement: Sputnik-
inspired cocktail ring
with topaz stones.*

*A starburst crystal
brooch from the 1960s.*

*1970s gold
and black chain.*

The quintessential wardrobe

Your dressing room, whether it's a walk-in closet or a row of cubbies, is a lot like a bar and should be well stocked with the essentials. Meaning, that sensational outfit, much like a crisp gin and tonic, must be readily accessible. Investing in classic, versatile pieces is the savviest way to build a trustworthy wardrobe. These are the separates and accessories that always enable you to dress and conquer—no matter how little time you have to get ready.

My list of "must-haves" comes from years of dressing different characters for every conceivable occasion, from business meetings to semiformal supper parties. I consider most of the following items to be investment pieces, so spend a bit more for deluxe fabrics and craftsmanship.

The top ten pieces every woman should own:

1 *A great pair of jeans:* Find the style that fits your body perfectly, whether it's a dark rinse, boot-leg cut, classic trouser, or skinny jean. If you can invest in only one pair, avoid über-trends like acid wash, slashing, or whiskering.

2 *Tailored blazer:* Choose a cut that best suits your silhouette, like one with a nipped waist or a puff at the sleeve, and be sure to choose a fine fabric like velvet, corduroy, tweed, or gabardine. A well-tailored traditional men's-style blazer never goes out of fashion.

3 *Sleek pencil skirt:* It's the most flexible separate that not only creates an instant polished silhouette, but also pairs well with boots, pumps, sweaters, jackets, and blouses.

4 *Designer knee-high leather boots:* A quality pair in a versatile shade like brown or black will last a lifetime, so make this an investment purchase. Be mindful of choosing a heel and toe-box (round is roomier and less trendy than the pointed version) that matches your lifestyle.

5 *Fantastic coat:* Don't dismiss outerwear when creating your look. When you enter a party or event, it's the first impression you make. A simple fitted pea coat can be embellished with a brooch; a classic satin swing coat in a bright color works with jeans or formal wear.

6 *Modern-day dress:* A smart, sleeveless shift or a lively wrap dress that's suitable for the office or a luncheon will work overtime if you add high-impact accessories like stilettos come nightfall.

7 *Sexy cocktail dress:* Not necessarily in black, this frock is your tried-and-true uniform, be it a sheath or a strapless mini, for any special occasion.

8 *Classic cardigan:* Both practical and sophisticated, the button-front sweater adds some elegance to day or nightwear and can be worn as a wrap. You can opt for any style, from the traditional cut to longer lengths.

9 *T-shirts:* It's impossible to layer without a few soft cotton tees that look so chic beneath a bouclé jacket or long, skinny sweater with leggings or a mini. Styles vary widely in color, length, fit, and necklines, so stock up on a few variations. A great tee can easily and inexpensively update a look.

10 *A pair of chic shoes from the current season:* A trendy pair of suede peep toes or platform sandals can enliven and refresh dated looks.

Dream a little dream

You can learn a lot about a woman just by peeking into her dressing room. A girl with frothy cocktail frocks hanging in her closet always finds her way to a lively party. The woman whose wardrobe consists mostly of skirt suits and tasteful pumps already has at least one toe in the corner office. Take a peek at your wardrobe and you can probably divine your lifestyle from the outfits and accessories you own.

Of course, it's important to build a wardrobe that complements those circumstances. After reading scripts for my characters, I create costumes appropriate to their professions, social habits, and general life situations. You can do the same by taking a close look at your work and social calendar for the past two or three months. Make note of how many dinner parties or business lunches or formal soirées you attended. Then, cross-reference that list of events with the contents of your closet. Maybe a recent promotion or career change has prompted a new itinerary of high-powered powwows. Or perhaps a new relationship has you attending charity galas and art openings. Be mindful that you should invest in clothes that suit your latest identity.

Practicalities aside, it's important to consider the transformative powers of fashion. I happen to collect bikinis in all colors, shapes, and styles because traveling to far-flung, remote beaches is a perennial life goal. Whenever I open my drawer of swimsuits, that aspiration comes to mind. (By the way, I now have enough bikinis to circle the globe and lounge on almost every shore.) If you're striving to revitalize your social calendar or working toward a promotion, start amassing pieces that will serve as further inspiration. They don't call them party dresses or power suits for nothing, after all.

» Traveling to far-flung, remote beaches is a perennial life goal. Whenever I open my drawer of swimsuits, that aspiration comes to mind.

It's all in the flow

Every principal character on *Mad Men* has a "costume closet." To simplify the process, all of their garments and accessories are neatly laid out according to the order in which they get dressed. For the women, bras and slips and other foundation garments like girdles are situated up front. This way, I can first outfit a character like Betty in the underclothes most appropriate for her ensemble. Blouses, skirts, suits, dresses, and then coats on hangers all follow. Then accessories like shoes, scarves, and jewelry sets of pearl or rhinestone necklaces and matching earrings come last. Thanks to this linear flow, I can quickly visualize each character's complete look from start to finish.

In my own closet, I apply the same principle by grouping my pieces in a succession that suits my approach to building an outfit. Even if you have a small closet you can arrange your pieces in categories. Being a fiend for accessories, I own a cabinet specially designated for all of my jewelry. Bangles, necklaces, earrings, and brooches each have their own compartments. You can always separate your accessories in a jewelry box that features divided nooks. My

wall of shoes, with over 100 pairs of high heels, comes next. (Clearly, I believe that a sensational stiletto can be the seed of a great look.) No matter how many pairs of shoes you own, it's smart to stack them in one area of your closet and even separate them according to "dressy" or "casual." Nearby are racks of separates like jeans and blouses and jackets, alongside day dresses and evening gowns. Coats nestle with other outerwear, and my clutches and purses are shelved in the back of my closet.

Next time you get dressed, record how you put together an outfit. If you start with a skirt or jeans and build upward, organize your racks in that visual order. Developing your own "costume closet" system will personalize the structure of your closet and make it easier to create fabulous outfits.

My 1960s amber bead necklace with a faceted topaz crystal closure.

The closet coup

Still hoarding a seasons-old skirt that just takes up space or sling-backs that chafe your heels? Set aside an afternoon for a wardrobe purge. Sentimental items like family heirlooms or cherished pieces that you can't part with because of their exemplary craftsmanship and fabrication can be stored separately.

Questions to ask before you start editing:

When did I last wear it? If it's been two years since you donned the suede miniskirt, that's over 700 days you went without it. Time to donate it to a local charity.

Does it fit right now? You shouldn't hoard a pair of jeans that now compromises your circulation or a dress that you've outgrown. If a garment no longer fits and can't be resized by a tailor, let it go and replace it with one that you can wear tonight.

Is it in need of repair or cleaning? Put items that are on hiatus because of their condition in a side pile and refer to the two-year rule. A purse with a strap that recently broke goes to the cobbler. The cashmere sweater with the marinara sauce stain that will never come out from your 2003 trip to Capri gets jettisoned.

Can I salvage it? If a beloved item can no longer be worn because it's too outdated but boasts an amazing print or expensive, sumptuous fabric, you may be able to recycle it. Bring it to a tailor, who can advise on possibilities.

Is it valuable? If you own designer or vintage pieces that are in excellent condition, have them appraised by a local consignor.

A contemporary rhinestone and enamel cocktail ring.

» *If you own designer or vintage pieces that are in excellent condition, have them appraised by a local consignor.*

Write your personal style bible

Getting dressed always requires a basic sense of direction. Beforehand, you might even ask yourself: "Where am I going with my look today and how do I get there?" Now imagine that your closet came with its own GPS and gently prodded you to pair the gray suede platform ankle boots with the tweed pencil skirt and long-sleeved tee when you punched in your style destination. Amazing, right?

Well, until someone invents such a wondrous device, you can more than make do with a fashion journal. Think of it as your personal style diary that details your favorite pieces and best looks. For on-set wardrobes, I keep track of which ensembles work best for certain characters as a referral for future outfits.

To create your own fashion journal, earmark either a notebook or a computer folder as a style bible. I prefer a small, handy notebook because you can jot down notes whenever you feel inspired and take it with you when you shop. Here you will keep a running dialogue on which outfits in your closet always make you feel confident and gorgeous. Think of the ones that fetch compliments, too.

When you play dress-up and experiment, you can write down which new combinations to try next. If a certain outfit craves a wide belt and you own just a skinny one, make a note for the next time you shop. The same goes for a broken heel or a fallen hem that requires repair.

THERE'S NO BETTER WAY TO MAKE A STATEMENT THAN TO OPT FOR A MATERIAL THAT LITERALLY SHINES ON ITS OWN

1. imperial silk metallic gold/black brocade 2. hot pink silk satin 3. black chantilly lace 4. silk floral print taffeta 5. khadi stripe metallic 6. polyester charmeuse leopard print 7. metallic violet brocade 8. metallic jacquard lamé

My favorite fabrics

Brocade, leather, Lurex, and lace. I am an addict to what I like to call "party fabrics." Leading ladies can't blend in with the background, and there's no better way to make a statement than to opt for a material that literally shines on its own. In season three, I costumed Betty Draper in a blue brocade dress embroidered with gold and silver butterflies and gave her white leather opera gloves for a formal event. Of course she stood apart from all the other women at the event.

If you survey your closet and see only solid woolens or cottons, it's time to invest in a few pieces that create instant impact because of the rich, sumptuous fabric. (Shopping vintage is a great way to score plush fabrics like silk charmeuse or brocade for less. In Chapter 5 we'll cover vintage in all its glory.) Find a bold fabric that speaks to you. Leather pants may flit in and out of style, but a sleek, fitted leather jacket is a perennial must. Same goes for a few metallic separates like gold ballet flats or silver Lurex sweaters.

» I always have an arsenal of pieces in my closet, like a vintage sequin dress and halter top.

Don't get me started on sequins. I always have an arsenal of pieces in my closet, like a vintage sequin dress and halter top. One of my go-to outfits is a sequined camisole with skinny jeans and high heels for a modernized take that seventies disco look. And why not add a faux fur jacket? (Quick caveat: Know that because sequins are reflective, they can add pounds. You can always opt to accessorize with a sequined belt or beret.) Show up in a sequined party dress and you'll definitely make a grand, sparkling entrance.

FABRICS VERSUS FIBERS

Confusion abounds when it comes to the difference between fabrics and fibers. Fibers or threads like wool or silk become fabrics or textiles like crepe or satin. I find the history of natural fibers to be fascinating. To create silk, filaments from the cocoon of a silkworm (a blind, flightless moth) are bound to make threads. This lustrous fiber dates back to China in about 2,500 B.C., and the wife of an emperor invented the loom. For thousands of years the country fiercely guarded its methods for producing silk, but the monopoly dissolved with immigration to India, Korea, and the Middle East. One story has it that monks smuggled silkworm eggs out of China in their walking staffs; another claims that a Chinese princess hijacked the precious eggs in her giant hairpiece.

Here's a quick timeline of the history of the most widely used natural and man-made fibers:

Natural Fibers

5,000 B.C.:
Flax, the oldest fiber, was woven to make linen and cloak Egyptian pharaohs for burial.

3,000 B.C.:
First cultivated in Pakistan and India, *cotton* is still the most popular fiber found in textiles today.

3,000 B.C.:
Wool, spun from the fleece of sheep, became the cloth of choice for Europeans during Roman times. Incidentally, cashmere and mohair come from goats; angora is shorn from rabbits.

2,500 B.C.:
As described above, *silk* is discovered in China and immediately becomes a treasured fabric.

Man-Made Fibers

1910:
Once known as "mother-in-law silk" because of its similarities to the natural fiber, *rayon* comes from wood pulp and was first developed by European chemists before being produced in the U.S.

1935:
Originally used for toothbrush bristles, *nylon* was later introduced in stockings in 1940. DuPont nearly named it "no-run" but didn't want to be legally held to such a heady claim.

1950:
Though developed a decade earlier in Britain, *polyester* hit the U.S. market midcentury and was embraced for its wrinkle resistance and durability.

1959:
Originally conceived as a replacement for rubber, *spandex* quickly became a staple fiber for sportswear because of its elasticity, fit, and comfort.

Lights-out luxe

There's no reason to retire glamour at the end of the evening. Why would you hang up a chic cocktail dress only to slip into frayed boxer shorts and an oversized T-shirt? Every woman, whether she's single or married or sharing a bed with a standard poodle, should own a gorgeous piece of nightwear for sleeping in style.

Betty Draper's frothy peignoirs may be too over-the-top for your taste. Still, you have to admit that she looks unbelievably elegant at the crack of dawn. You can achieve the same effect with a chemise or a pair of silk charmeuse pajamas à la Katharine

Hepburn. A quilted satin robe with peak lapels is equally sophisticated. For a more gamine effect, try a lacy teddy or satin tap pants with a matching camisole.

Long or short vintage silk kimonos also add a little kick to any sleepwear. (Vintagekimono.com sells stunning silk jacquard robes in all different lengths.) I have a collection of delicious little slippers and fancy robes, but my standout piece is a hot pink, full-length silk charmeuse robe with a rhinestone-studded sash that doubles as an eye mask. Yes, a bedazzled eye mask. Good night.

Cocktail CHATTER

WHO HAD THE BIGGER CLOSET, CLEOPATRA OR EVITA?
Well, Elizabeth Taylor held the record for the most wardrobe changes—65 in total—when she filmed the epic *Cleopatra* in 1963 with Renié as costume designer. But Madonna dethroned her with 85 costume changes in *Evita* in 1996. Incidentally, the Material Girl's wardrobe included 39 hats, 45 pairs of shoes, and 56 pairs of earrings, all overseen by costume designer Penny Rose.

OVER 450 MILLION PAIRS OF JEANS ARE PURCHASED EVERY YEAR IN THE UNITED STATES, and the average American woman has seven of them in her closet. In 2005, an anonymous eBay bidder paid $60,000 for a 155-year-old pair of Levi's 501s.

MARIE ANTOINETTE DREW ENOUGH IRE FOR HER OPULENT FASHIONS THAT CROWDS STORMED HER DRESSING ROOM at the Tuileries palace in Paris to loot or destroy her garments. Another mob smashed all the mirrors in her closet at Versailles.

CHECKLIST

Earmark a weekend afternoon to loot your own closet and experiment with new combinations. Be sure to include accessories in this game of dress-up.

Start a fashion journal and record your most basic info: measurements, shoe size, most flattering colors and silhouettes, shopping needs. Jot down your favorite outfits as you discover them.

Do an inventory of your wardrobe essentials and please try on your jeans, cocktail dress, and blazer to ensure that each still fits perfectly.

Purge that closet and invite three friends over for a clothing swap. Ask each one to bring her most fashionable discards and recycle. Serve snacks and a crisp Sancerre.

Appraise the system you use to organize your closet and gauge its efficiency. If you don't yet have a system, go back and reread this chapter immediately.

DRESSING
CHIC for every
OCCASION

4

How we dress harkens back to our upbringing. When I was growing up in the South, femininity always trumped functionality. Women got gussied up and applied a full face of makeup before their first sip of coffee. To leave the house undone was a social misdemeanor. The young Bryant girls all wore pastel-colored coats with matching hats and gloves as white as a new bar of soap.

In fact, I wore a dress every single day of my life up until sixth grade. (For active afternoons on the jungle gym, my ensemble included a pair of shorts hidden beneath the frilly skirt.) Why would a little girl so vehemently avoid pants? Credit my great-aunt Kate, a woman who never revealed her age because such a taboo topic was never broached. She told me that trousers on a woman were "rude." Yes, rude. Incidentally, Aunt Kate was an amazing woman who graduated from the Teachers College at Columbia University in the 1920s. She also taught me how to draw my first models, which were elegant Asian women because I was obsessed with Chinese and Japanese culture and fashion at the age of five. It's still easy for me to picture her fiery red hair and cat-eye glasses, which magnified her cornflower blue eyes to the size of silver dollars. Of course not everyone has an Aunt Kate, but think back to your childhood and recall those who inspired you in some way.

Nowadays, of course, my wardrobe includes many pairs of trousers and lots of denim. (Don't look, Aunt Kate.) But the notion of always presenting a polished image wafts around me like the scent of gardenias whenever I choose an outfit. Though it may not be customary to dress up for a doctor appointment or for flying across the country, I still do. Even my most casual getup would pass muster with my mother. I also throw black-tie dinner parties and thrill to see my guests decked out like proud peacocks. Think of your outfits as a dress code for life and get ready every morning with a vengeance.

A spoonful of style medicine

Outfit anxiety. This stressful fashion disorder can strike when you don't prepare an amazing complete look for an important occasion. Symptoms: difficulty breathing, racing heartbeat, and a sudden onset of agoraphobia, or fear of leaving the house. In my job, I skirt this dreaded condition—known on the set as "costume anxiety"—by dutifully planning out each look for my characters. Once a script arrives, it's time to page through and designate the right ensemble (from the pearl earrings to the garters) for every scene.

If Peggy Olson has a major presentation for clients at the agency, you can bet I create a suitable costume with some added panache like her blue linen two-piece suit with the self-piping. But my dogged foresight doesn't stop there. On an index card I also jot down all of her undergarments and accessories, right down to the purse she will carry to that big meeting. Such preparations also allow me to plan out each episode and get a sense of the color schemes of all of my characters.

If you are prone to the occasional fashion panic attack—and, really, who isn't?—do employ this handy strategy at home. You're best off assessing your options a few days before a momentous event so you have some time to shop or dry-clean an item, if need be. Once you settle on a fantastic outfit, record the entire look in your fashion journal and set all the pieces aside. Be sure to include the proper undergarments and even accessories.

When I travel, I try to plan out each outfit to avoid overpacking. My luggage always contains a few extra options like alternative blouses or extra jackets and a slew of light accessories like belts and jewelry, which can change up a look. No vacation should ever be sullied by a bout of outfit anxiety.

» *Once you settle on a fantastic outfit, record the entire look in your fashion journal and set all the pieces aside.*

Comfort versus chic

Just as the right accessories can enliven any outfit, the wrong pieces will surely maim a stylish silhouette. I refer to these items as "fashion felons" and can guarantee that they never play nice with other separates. Sneakers, for instance, are appropriate only for athletics. And don't think that you can get away with them while running errands. You can find a smart, chic alternative that's equally easy on the feet. Skeptical? Read on.

Fashion felon

A SHAPELESS TEE

The white T-shirt, first issued by the navy, was originally designed as an undershirt beneath a uniform. But ever since the fifties it has become an American staple and tripled in size. (I'm not talking about the huge, trendy tees with shoulder pads from the eighties, either.) If you're swimming in a T-shirt, your silhouette suddenly appears as vast as the ocean. Toss this top or relegate it to attire for garden work or attic cleaning.

Stylish substitute

You needn't banish tees. Just be sure to find a style that doesn't swallow you whole, and opt for little feminine accents like a puffed sleeve or a low ballet back. Ruching on the sides will slim your outline and three-quarter sleeves are always flattering. Experiment with varied necklines like a V, cowl, or boatneck style. A cotton tunic is just as breathable as a tee. Plus you get a wink at your natural curves and femininity.

Fashion felon

THE SWEATSUIT

Or any pair of sweat pants that puckers at the waist and adds unnecessary bulk to the midriff. You also forfeit self-awareness of your shape, which can lead to unhealthy eating. Eliminate these pants from your day-to-day wardrobe unless you are wearing them during exercise or while lounging at home.

Stylish substitute

Linen drawstring pants—a favorite staple of mine—deliver comfort and definition. A well-fitted pair of jeans or even silk parachute pants can be paired with a flattering T-shirt and flat boots to complete your new look. Don't forget to add some accessories like a gold cuff or enamel bangles.

Fashion felon

VISIBLE PANTY LINES

These pesky undergarment outlines disrupt the flow of a tailored silhouette. Plus they hardly flatter the backside. Similarly, a protruding panty strap looks more unkempt than alluring.

Stylish substitute

The thong—originally worn by men more than 50,000 years ago as a loincloth—is one handy solution for eradicating panty lines. If you're averse to the style, girdle-inspired shapewear will certainly do the trick.

Fashion felon

DISHEVELED SNEAKERS

Perhaps the perpetually chic Parisians abhor jogging because it would force them to wear running shoes? A pair of slipshod sneakers, with scuff marks or grass stains, should be worn only for athletic reasons or to a sporting event. In my opinion, they defy femininity.

Stylish substitute

Flat-heeled boots, ballet flats, summer sandals, and espadrilles all make perfect alternatives. Or try a pair of slip-on canvas skimmers in a vivid red, green, or floral print, which look cute with jeans, shorts, or even a summer mini dress.

Fashion felon

VISIBLE PROTRUDING MIDRIFFS, AKA MUFFIN-TOPS, AND BRA BACK BULGES

Again, these disruptions to your contours break up that natural long line of the body.

Stylish substitute

If you're not blessed with a slim torso, replace low-rise jeans with a high-waisted style that doesn't pinch at the midriff. A well-fitted bra should eradicate back bulges, or try Spanx's Bra-llelujah with a hosiery back and elastic-free straps that create a smooth, invisible effect.

Shapewear to the rescue. A sexy, control undergarment: Flexees by Maidenform boudoir slip.

Retail therapy

All this talk of attire may inspire you to rethink your wardrobe and even hightail it to a boutique or department store. Bravo. But do know that there is a dress code for a shopping excursion, too. Simply put, look great. Over the years, I have learned that I make the best fashion choices when I look fantastic and feel confident. I'm much more adventurous in my selections. Wear a favorite outfit that always instills you with verve; bolster your look and attitude with some effort spent on hair and makeup. Just think about how many times you saunter past a full-length mirror and never mind those obnoxious fluorescent lights.

Clearly, you want to wear an ensemble that slips on and off easily, and be sure to tote along a pair of heels if you're browsing for a party dress or more formal wear. Heels make me feel better. Bring along shapewear that will finesse your silhouette, if need be. Same goes for proper undergarments, like a strapless bra. Last, don't forget that you're always on a mission to experiment with your style. Make it a point to try on at least three pieces that spur you to think, "I would never wear that." Eye the racks and counters with an entirely fresh perspective. Which items feel too bold or perhaps even too fashion forward? Never tried on a sequined jumpsuit or a lace bustier? The time is now.

Day-to-day wear

Each and every day is an opportunity to dress well and show off your unique sense of style. Often women become flustered about the attire for a special occasion because they forgo effort on their daily appearance. If you're accustomed to wearing overly casual togs, dressing for a semiformal luncheon or dinner party suddenly feels daunting. It's a long leap from your comfort zone, no pun intended. But if you regularly maintain a high standard on the image you present, it's much simpler to elevate that look to the next level for an event.

Betty Draper never sacrifices personal style. She dons her lustrous pearls and shirtwaist dress whether she's ironing or entertaining. As *Mad Men*'s makeup artist Lana Horchowski says, "The housewives in the 1960s would manicure their nails to wash the dishes." Of course, many of those nonworking women had a surplus of time to ready themselves and to deliberate between the lizard pumps or the patent-leather slingbacks. I'll take our more harried but fulfilling modern-day lives, thank you.

Still, even a quick spurt of devotion to detail can make a noticeable difference. An easy way to approach day-to-day style is to think of your look as a uniform. That doesn't mean monotony, though. Rather, you want to isolate a simple look that works for you and assemble a few outfits in that vein. If you adore day dresses, buy a couple of them for dashing out to a luncheon or a last-minute invitation to a barbecue. If you're more comfortable in separates, find a cut of pants or jeans that flatters you and a top that also complements your frame.

Here are my top six tips for achieving a professional and chic style:

1 *Focus on the fit.* Impeccable tailoring will add a more polished and luxurious edge to trousers, jackets, skirts, and blouses. Most dry cleaners offer simple alterations for less than twenty dollars.

2 *Dress up a rung or two from your current job.* In other words, outfit yourself for the position you desire.

3 *Take a cue from the corner office.* To get a sense of the dress code at a new office, look to your superior and mirror her level of style. If your boss always wears skirt suits with heels, match her level of professionalism with sharp separates.

4 *Rely on accessories to express yourself.* Colorful belts, bold metallic cuffs, and statement shoes or bags will animate any conservative suit. Just avoid overdoing it with jewelry like bangles or dangling earrings that tinkle when you move.

5 *Avoid showing an abundance of skin.* Cleavage and extremely short skirts may garner lustful gazes, but they won't get you a promotion.

6 *Travel in style.* Be mindful of attire on business trips—even when you fly—as you are still representing your company.

» *Colorful belts, bold metallic cuffs, and statement shoes or bags will animate any conservative suit.*

My Peruvian hand-tooled leather clutch; a 1980s ornate belt that enlivens any outfit.

Nine-to-five and beyond

While workplaces may vary wildly in style, one requirement for dressing the part remains constant. Look professional—from every angle. That hardly means you must renounce your personal style to appear polished. In fact, injecting some personal flair into your work attire telegraphs both confidence and creativity.

On *Mad Men*, the secretaries of Sterling Cooper wear dresses or skirts and hosiery, which was an absolute must. (In fact, sales of pantyhose only started declining in the mid-nineties, when many companies relaxed their corporate dress codes for women.) But most of the secretaries who work at the fictional ad agency still indulge their personalities with color and accessories like brooches and hats and handbags. Joan Holloway never strides through the office pool without her trusty gold pen dangling from a chain around her neck. I love that accessory because the accent exudes authority and utilitarian elegance.

> » *Joan Holloway never strides through the office pool without her trusty gold pen dangling from a chain around her neck. I love that accessory because the accent exudes authority and utilitarian elegance.*

The dress-down dilemma

Casual Fridays? Sorry, but I just don't believe in them. Can you imagine Peggy Olson wearing Bermuda shorts to Sterling Cooper? Or Don Draper making a presentation in a pair of ratty sneakers? What you wear says so much about you, and people constantly form first impressions based on appearances—no matter the day of the week.

When it comes to denim, opt for a tailored trouser cut in a dark rinse. It's much more formal than faded or whiskered denim. No holes or fraying, naturally. To be prepared for an impromptu important meeting, keep a sophisticated tailored jacket on hand. A chic bouclé blazer can dress up any outfit in a pinch. It doesn't hurt to stow a pair of heels in a file drawer, either.

Inside the trunk of my car, you'll find a mobile closet. I store three pairs of heels, including a pair of gold pumps, jeans, a blouse, and my favorite little black dress. A 1970s yellow felt floppy hat and my belly-dancing outfit are nestled back there, too. Clearly, I'm always prepared for a cocktail party —in Cairo.

Again and again

Opinions abound when it comes to repeating outfits. Red carpet–trotting starlets may refuse to wear the same frock twice, but the modern woman can certainly be seen in the same getup every now and again. On *Mad Men*, I might repeat a certain look to foster continuity or even familiarity for the audience. You feel closer to a character when you recognize her dress or coat from a previous episode. Obviously, the characters have emotional ties to their clothes, too.

For example, Betty Draper favors a goldenrod yellow cardigan with a lace front that she has donned in all three seasons. It's her mainstay sweater. Peggy wore a blue-and-black-checked drop-waisted dress during season one and then at the very outset of season two. She even chose it for the day she went in to ask Don Draper for a raise, so you know it's her bravado outfit.

Right now, my go-to look consists of a favorite pair of skinny jeans, high-heeled boots, and a fitted leather jacket. I may repeat the ensemble every so often, but I always change up the overall effect with a completely different belt or a radical shift in jewelry. (See the seven ways to transform a little black dress into a fresh look in Chapter 6.) It's best to reinvent the in go-to look every three months so you don't end up in a fashion rut.

My only caveat for outfit repetition is this: Wearing the same formal gown to events where you might be photographed, whether they be family occasions or charity galas, can become awkward if you're pictured in the same dress over and over again. My friends and I gown-swap when we're seeking new black-tie options. Who wants to borrow my lilac silk chiffon Valentino?

Enchanted evenings

Nothing thrills me like a watercolor-worthy sunset and an evening plan. Nighttime events, from cocktail parties to concerts to formal galas, offer the ultimate chance to show off your style IQ and take some fashion risks.

» *A sea of funereal black dresses saddens the paparazzi to no end. Explore gowns in jewel tones or pastel hues if you're usually more inclined to darker shades.*

The Gala

From walking the red carpets at the Emmys, I have learned that photographers love color. It naturally draws the eye. A sea of funereal black dresses saddens the paparazzi to no end. Explore gowns in jewel tones or pastel hues if you're usually more inclined to darker shades. For shoes, a strappy nude or metallic heel easily lends itself to any color, cut, or style. Be sure to carry an evening purse, whether it's a slim envelope style or a miniature frame bag with a thin shoulder strap.

The Cocktail Soirée

This is one of my favorite events because there are so many fun directions to go with a party dress. Options are endless when it comes to fabric (tulle, organza, lace, silk charmeuse, satin, and jersey) and length, from mini to tea length and everything in between. Bring out your high-impact accessories, too. Big bulky bags weigh down an evening look, so opt for a sophisticated smaller purse.

The Dinner Party

I think of my mother whenever I throw a dinner party. As the ultimate hostess, she always served fondue while wearing her floral Lilly Pulitzer maxi dresses and her tinkling gold charm bracelet. There was no mistaking the Bryant girls, as we all wore little dresses matched to her ensemble. Now my preferred getup is something flowy, like my jumpsuit with a halter top and dramatic Moroccan coral necklace that allows me to dash around to greet guests without looking frazzled. To avoid an outfit upset in the kitchen, add a flirty vintage organza apron. My grandmother owned a collection of aprons, which now gets put to good use on *Mad Men*. Betty Draper donned one of my grandmother's adorable pink-and-green brocade aprons when she entertained Don's colleagues.

The First Date

The most important rule is to radiate confidence. Pick an outfit that doesn't leave you uncertain at all, and avoid anything too revealing. But keep in mind that it's always good to provide a hint of temptation, so opt for a dress or a skirt rather than jeans or pants.

This adorable Judith Leiber minaudière will not be ignored.

The last word on weddings

Long before couples started uttering "I do" on surfboards or atop Mount Everest, wedding attire was hardly a conundrum. The time of the event dictated the dress code, and invites didn't specify "beach chic" or "dressy casual." An evening wedding always called for black tie; afternoon nuptials signified short dresses and suits. A female guest wearing black—or white, of course—was about as welcome as a hailstorm.

Nowadays, however, wedding attire has evolved to include a wide variety of possibilities, so much so that a guest might be instructed to wear "all white" or even "Goth glam." Black no longer strictly signifies mourning, so it's perfectly acceptable at a late-afternoon or evening affair. Still, I believe that a colorful palette adds to the festive spirit. So I prefer to see women in softer shades like pale blues, purples, corals, and hues of pink. After all, a wedding is a perfect occasion to toast love and romance with the most feminine of fashion.

Wearing red to a wedding, by the way, was once a sure sign that you were a husband-heisting Jezebel. This is no longer the case, thankfully. But anything overly sexy (neckline to the navel) or super slinky (side slit to the upper thigh) is never appropriate. Similarly, an overly dramatic cupcake of a dress with tulle, tiers, and rosettes should be avoided. You never want to upstage the bride or be mistaken for a wedding cake.

These days, invitations either designate a dress code or offer no suggestion at all. Again, a wedding after five P.M. that doesn't call for black tie should be considered semiformal. Here are some modern-day style cues:

White tie: The pinnacle of posh, this event requires a knockout evening gown with high heels and an appropriately dainty purse like a satin clutch or minaudière. Jewels are strongly encouraged. You can even go all out with opera-length gloves to heighten the drama.

Black tie: An elegant full-length gown or ultra-dressy cocktail-length dress with standout beading or sequins works perfectly. Add chandelier earrings or a bejeweled cuff for more punch. If the invite specifies "black tie optional," it's more of a nudge to dress it up than a stated dress code.

Semiformal: Bypass the gown for a sophisticated cocktail dress with a pair of statement heels in a wow color or featuring embellishments like studs or embroidery. Add bold jewelry like a cocktail ring or dramatic drop earrings. An embroidered wrap or sparkly purse injects some panache, too.

Pavé 1970s diamond earrings, a present from my mother.

Formal day wedding: Opt for a skirt suit or dress in silk chiffon, a most feminine and frothy fabric that looks exceptional at afternoon nuptials. A headpiece, whether it's a bejeweled hair comb or a sprig of fresh flowers, always garners a few winks and smiles, too.

Semiformal day: Skip the sequins for a smart day dress like a sleeveless sheath in a vivid color or a printed silk dress with a full skirt. Palazzo pants with a silk blouse do the trick, too.

Informal: Don't mistake this directive for everyday casual. An informal wedding still calls for a put-together look like a simple dress or tailored slacks with a polished top. No flip-flops or denim or bare midriffs, of course. For a picnic wedding on a lawn, think sundress. Go with sandals or a wedge heel that won't leave you churning up clods of grass.

Beach: A diaphanous, flowing dress and sandals positively makes the grade. (If your sandals are high-heeled, carry them over your shoulder or in a cute tote.) Linen separates—accented with jewelry like assorted bangles or long ethnic beads—also add up to a sharp look. Beachwear like sarongs, bikini tops, shorts, and anything made of terry cloth are not appropriate—unless the ocean is the dance floor.

A flirty, floral confection suits the romantic mood of a wedding.

Cocktail CHATTER

IN HER DELIGHTFUL 1959 BOOK *THE DRESS DOCTOR*,
famed costume designer Edith Head prescribes the following attire for a
night at the movies: "Day or afternoon dress, or suit; + dress shoes + wrap
as needed. Gloves optional." For attending a circus, she recommends:
"Sport suit, sport dress, day dress, dress + jacket. Or skirt with blouse or
sweater. Comfortable street shoes. Hat and gloves optional. At night add
jacket or coat." Incidentally, Head was nominated for thirty-five Academy
Awards and won eight, more than any other woman.

HOSIERY'S LAST GASP?
In 2007, cosmetics queen
Mary Kay relented on her
professional attire guidelines
and made pantyhose and
closed-toe shoes "optional" at
company-sponsored events.

**THE TIME-HELD TRADITION OF
WEARING WHITE AS A BRIDE DATES
BACK ONLY TO 1840,** when Queen
Victoria married in a simple ivory
satin gown and matching veil
because she wanted to incorporate
Honiton lace into the look. Prior to
that storied wedding, brides wore
any color but black or red, and
royals typically donned ermine-
edged velvet or brocade finery
on the big day.

CHECKLIST

Take a peek at your social calendar for the next two weeks and
then plan a great outfit ahead of time for an upcoming important
presentation or meeting.

Assess your closet for fashion felons like sloppy sneakers or
baggy T-shirts and upgrade accordingly.

Stow a pair of fun heels in your trunk for last-minute invites
and stash a tailored jacket at the office for impromptu powwows
with VIPs.

Remember to tote necessary undergarments, shapewear,
and the proper shoes on future shopping excursions.

Throw a dinner party—why not?—and then treat yourself
to a flirty vintage apron that will wow your guests.

A PASSION for VINTAGE

Ah, vintage. Is it possible to be born with a keen love for gauntlet gloves from the 1930s and seventies-era polyester plaid pants threaded in your DNA? Shortly after learning to walk, I marched my way into my mother's childhood bedroom closet—at my grandmother's house—and became a gleeful two-foot-tall mannequin for her 1950s dresses, hats, and shoes. My fantasies of being a glamorous movie star were fulfilled when I slipped into layers of tulle and countless rhinestones. And that filigreed silver jewelry case I once plundered now holds my own collection of Victorian watch fobs, bejeweled brooches, beaded necklaces, and cocktail rings from all eras.

In my small town of Cleveland, Tennessee, my obsession with vintage blossomed into eccentric public spectacle. My tastes ran to full circle skirts from the 1950s, 1940s peplum jackets, and hand-sewn collars and bows from antique textiles. No wonder my older sister always called me "Miss Vogue" as I sashayed down the hallways of Cleveland High School. A midcentury strapless blue silk organza gown—with as many lace-overlay tiers as a wedding cake—made for the perfect dress when yours truly was crowned Horton Society Queen of the Riverside Military Academy. I also painfully pranced about in a beloved pair of my mother's blue pumps from the sixties that were a size too small and much too narrow for my growing feet. Blisters be damned!

For me, the appeal was as obvious as topstitching. Wearing vintage pieces enabled me to express my evolving style in a unique way. Today, I'm just as enamored with the inherent individuality of bygone garments and accessories. What are the odds that two women will wear the same 1960s cocktail dress to a party? About as slim as the cut of a pair of cigarette pants. Vintage instantly brings distinction to any outfit. It also telegraphs an appreciation for the rich history of fashion.

These days, when scouring for vintage for my own personal collection, my eye goes right to the details like the handiwork of an embroidered sweater or the construction of buttonholes. Examine a suit from the sixties and you might find chains sewn into the hems to weight the garment and ensure that it falls perfectly. Open a fabulous 1930s clutch and you'll likely see a pristine silk lining with matching comb, mirror, and change purse. These thoughtful particulars all speak to a long-forgotten devotion to quality that's hard to mimic in today's ready-to-wear clothes. Plus there's a certain sense of self-possession that comes with owning a creative and thoughtfully constructed garment. It's like wearing art. Never mind the fact that you can score vintage treasures for about a quarter of the price that you would spend on their contemporary counterparts.

Ready to join me in my obsession?

1980s bright green leather shoe clips.

A delicate 1950s floral brooch, perfect for a collar.

My favorite vintage pieces:
decade by decade

Nothing matches the exhilaration of pouncing upon an amazing vintage treasure like a rhinestone dress clip or a beaded cashmere sweater. The hunt itself can be as thrilling as the discovery. I love to prowl through a vintage shop or thrift store, foraging through racks and scouring shelves. But it also helps to have a target or a specific item in mind, especially as every decade produced varied silhouettes and styles attuned to the country's moods and cultural shifts.

Over the years, I have developed my own list of the best vintage pieces that date back to various periods. These items all marry effortlessly with modern looks, which is always key. And I like to think that my picks boast the most unique design and intricate craftsmanship of each era. Certain vintage stores even group their inventory according to decade, which makes it much easier to spot that 1930s crocodile envelope clutch or pair of oversized sunglasses from 1967. Good luck hunting. Unless I get there first, of course.

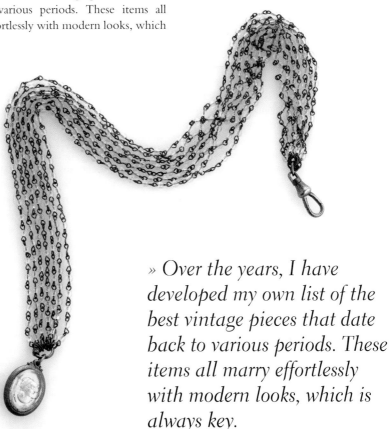

A 1960s chocolate diamond and mother-of-pearl cocktail ring, and my unique Victorian watch fob.

» *Over the years, I have developed my own list of the best vintage pieces that date back to various periods. These items all marry effortlessly with modern looks, which is always key.*

1920s

"Speakeasy Style"

The style sensibility

The flapper immediately comes to mind with mention of the Roaring Twenties, even though that sleek liberated icon didn't actually emerge until 1926. Still, during this period, women rejoiced in their independence and disdained any restrictions. Camisoles replaced corsets; hemlines crept above the knee. Sportswear became a fashion must, with jersey skirts and drop-waisted dresses making it easy to leap up and do the Charleston.

That verve extended into accessories in the form of boas, feathered headbands, and rhinestone-encrusted cigarette holders. Exotic influences borrowed from Asia, Egypt, Greece, and Mexico ended up in lamé embroidery, beaded designs, and colorful textiles.

The standout: 1920s

A BEADED EVENING BAG

These ornate purses are typically the size of a potholder (ten-or-twelve-by-seven inches) and will force you to streamline your necessities for a night out. Hundreds of glass beads make up distinctive designs that range from Art Deco–inspired floral motifs to rug patterns to chevrons and stripes. Look for the rare depictions of exotic locales like Egypt's pyramids or the Alps and any bags that feature a bottom fringe for some movement.

Every inch entails workmanship. Many of the frames are exquisitely detailed marcasite with a chain handle or faux tortoiseshell made from Bakelite. Clasps range from cabochons to whimsical touches like acorns or elephants. I love the old Whiting & Davis Co. enameled mesh purses, too.

Wear it with: The iridescent colors make these bags the perfect complement to a little black dress or even a wedding gown. But you can add some pizzazz to a pair of skinny jeans, high heels, and a bomber jacket, too. Just be sure to keep the outfit's color combination to a minimum so that the purse steals the spotlight.

Other treasures to seek out: Chic felt cloches, mandarin velvet coats with intricate embroidery, compacts, and long pearl necklaces.

1930ˢ

"The Era of Eros"

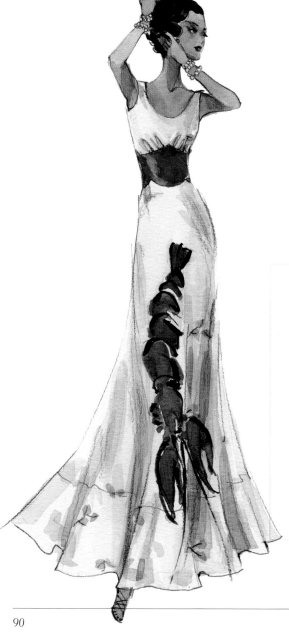

The style sensibility

The woman as androgynous minx gave way to an ovation to femininity. Rounded busts and defined waistlines came back in vogue, along with sculpted shoulders and backless gowns. (Sunbathing was all the rage, thanks to swimsuits that didn't cover every square inch of skin, and ladies wanted to show off that sun-kissed glow.)

Famed Paris fashion designer Madeleine Vionnet cross-cut fabrics on the bias—at a diagonal to caress curves—and added draping and ruching that transformed women into Grecian goddesses. Italian designer Elsa Schiaparelli's surreal looks, such as the lobster gown with a crustacean painted on the skirt by Salvador Dali (left), and penchant for shocking pink made fashion a high-impact sport.

The standout: 1930s

VINTAGE WEDDING GOWNS

I'm obsessed with wedding gowns from this decade because they celebrate grace and femininity by skimming a woman's curves and feature a long, sleek silhouette. Look for bias-cut silk satin gowns that button down the back or close at the side and accents like lace or ruched sleeves or self-belts that cinch with a rhinestone clasp. They are perfect for a black-tie event. To avoid looking like a newlywed, add colorful accents like a bright red clutch or vividly hued shoes. (Incidentally, wedding dresses were designed with removable trains so that women could have them dyed for future occasions.) »

Costume jewelry, which was popularized back in this era and designed to complement one particular outfit, also makes a great find. Some women even disposed of a piece after wearing it. Coco Chanel called it "junk jewelry." Glass, base metals like nickel or brass, plastic like Lucite, and stones replaced precious materials.

You'll find jewelry from both the Art Deco and Retro Period (post-1935) that dates back to the thirties. Geometric patterns like circles and triangles mark the Deco lot, with lots of black-and-white enamel and motifs of autos, planes, sphinxes (King Tut's tomb had been discovered in 1922), and panthers. Look for bangles, long pendants, rhinestone dress clips, and cocktail rings.

The Retro Period, marked by a return to curves and more femininity in design, produced pieces with flower, bow, fruit, dog, and horse motifs. Keep an eye out for the florid Bakelite brooches in primary colors or bangles with gradations in hues.

Wear it with: High-heeled sandals add modern contrast to the vintage wedding dress. Carry a contemporary clutch or sparkly minaudière. With regards to the jewelry, Bakelite or brass brooches dress up a jacket or sweater, and colorful bangles add punch to a little black dress. If you purchase a set, be sure to wear items as separates and mix in modern accessories like hoops or layered chains.

Other treasures to seek out: Capelets, bias-cut velvet dresses with draping shoulder details and matching jackets, Lucite and Bakelite purses with brass or rhinestone accents.

1940ˢ

*"Patriotism
& Peplum"*

The style sensibility

The Second World War profoundly affected every aspect of fashion, from color to cuts to fabrics. Austerity reined in design and hues; frills brought frowns of disapproval. Women had to rely on bright red lipstick and cascades of curls as substitutes for sartorial frippery. With a shortage of silk, they drew lines down the backs of their legs to mimic seamed stockings. Hemlines hit knee lengths on straight skirts, and shoulder pads helped to create a silhouette. The rare nod to style was the peplum, that wave of fabric bordering the bottom of a short jacket, which helped add contours.

Come 1947, with the war finished, women hungered for a fresh direction in fashion. Thankfully, Christian Dior sated that yen and introduced the New Look, a collection that accentuated full hips, prominent shoulders, and a tiny, nipped waist with bustier bodices, padding, and petticoats. His liberal use of fabrics for each design was a tongue wag to wartime shortages.

The standout: 1940s
ARCHITECTURAL HATS

Mod sculptural and architectural hats, which were a fashion staple in the 1940s because all that rationing restricted fabrics and materials used for clothes. These whimsical accessories, often festooned with flowers, fur, and feathers, became the antidote to wartime utilitarian wear, and the designs are outrageously fun. You can be sure that I would have been a collector back then.

You won't be overlooked in a toque adorned with ostrich feathers or in one of the soft, ruched velvet turbans of the period. I adore the stiff, swooped felt designs that perch atop the head like punctuation marks. Talk about jaunty. Or the black straw wide-brimmed hats with flattering upturned brims. Look for felt flowers and rolled brims, as well as beading and sequins. With the variety of shapes, sizes, and adornments, you can find one that best suits your personality.

Wear it with: You want to contrast this vintage flourish with a contemporary look. A tailored blazer with skinny jeans or a miniskirt and high heels makes a great match.

Other treasures to seek out: Alligator and lizard bags, peplum jackets, crocheted clutches, high-waisted palazzo-style pants in Polynesian prints, and rayon jersey dresses.

1950<u>s</u>

"Optimism Invades Fashion"

The style sensibility

Enter the hourglass—and the merciless undergarments necessary to achieving curves that drew wolf whistles. The iconic form-fitting sheath dress, as worn by bombshells like Marilyn Monroe, epitomized style and a refreshingly frank sensuality in fashion. Post-war optimism had already muscled out stoicism, and fashion followed suit with crinoline skirts and voluminous coats and dresses that crooned of excess.

Women now sought the most elegant and ladylike effects. Outfits featured matched sets of purses, hats, and shoes. (Salvatore Ferragamo and Roger Vivier have been credited with inventing the stiletto in the early 1950s.) Gloves were a must-have accessory for day and evening. Chanel's wildly popular collarless boxy jacket and straight skirt suits spawned a legion of mass-produced impostors. Meanwhile, teen girls stopped dressing like their mothers and flaunted their youth in poodle skirts and high ponytails. Of all the periods, the fifties ranks as one of my favorites because of the opulence and exaggerated shapes that marked the era. The jeweled buttons, tulle, and ruffles all exulted in femininity.

The standout: 1950s

A CIRCLE SKIRT

A circle skirt, that midcentury staple that flatters with its cinched waist and flare at the hips. Traditionally, the garment is actually made from just one piece of fabric with a hole cut in the center, hence the name. I love the way these gems sway and swirl when you walk or turn. In *Roman Holiday,* Audrey Hepburn rides a Vespa and traipses around the city in a feminine circle skirt paired with a simple white blouse and jaunty neck scarf.

I'm forever searching for ones that tell a little story. You can find patterns that feature a travel motif (maps, luggage, or a far-flung landscape) or a sly border print of martinis and pink elephants. Some circle skirts even have hand-sewn designs made up of crystals, beads, and jewels. Look for skirts imported from Mexico emblazoned with bold colorful flowers or desert scenes with cacti and sunsets.

Wear it with: I like to pair my circle skirts with a sweet, short-sleeved button-down blouse à la Hepburn. Be sure to add a belt to cinch the waist further. Sleek pumps or sandals work well, as you want a simple shoe that won't detract from the girly silhouette.

Other treasures to seek out: High-collared blouses with ruffles and pearl buttons, embroidered cashmere cardigans, strapless layered tulle dresses with tea-length skirts.

My vintage poodle pin: perfect for a lapel or sweater.

1960ˢ

"The Mod Revolution"

The style sensibility

Fashions well reflect the social turbulence and cool artistic influences of this decade. In the earlier years, before the sixties started to swing, graceful and genteel Jackie Kennedy led women to favor slim-cut suits, candy-colored shifts, swing coats, and pillbox hats. The looks are a natural extension of the 1950s, with elegance and domesticity as a central theme.

About mid-decade, however, the fashion pendulum pivoted toward a revolution fueled by technology and youth culture. Brit Mary Quant popularized the shocking miniskirt, which had been invented by designer André Courrèges. (By the way, the name comes from an abbreviation for "minimum.") Pierre Cardin, inspired by space missions, introduced futuristic jumpers and dresses with vinyl panels. Op art overtook prints, with splashy colors and mind-bending geometrics showing up on minis and pantsuits. The style evolution took yet another turn when the hippie movement emerged at the era's tail end.

The standout: 1960s
A GO-ANYWHERE CAPE

A go-anywhere cape, which adds some chic and mystique to any outfit. What could be more mod than a deconstructed coat? The lengths vary from a hem that falls mid-torso to long, sweeping styles with a more romantic bent.

You can opt for a smart woven woolen version in tweed, herringbone, or plaid. The double-breasted ones offer just the right wink at masculinity. I look for leather piping and distinctive buttons or draped funnel-neck collars. Many feature slit pockets or side arms that make them more practical for daily doings, like carrying a purse or driving a car.

Wear it with: A simple knit top and leggings or a mini with knee-high or ankle boots. You want to create some definition below the knee to balance the silhouette.

Other treasures to seek out: Square-toed patent-leather shoes with flourishes like buckles or flowers on the toe and matching purses, cocktail dresses, and bug-eyed sunglasses.

1970ˢ

"Gypsies, Hippies,
& the Hustle"

The style sensibility

The radical flower-child looks of the late sixties bled into the early 1970s. Women wore fringed suede miniskirts one day and flowered maxi dresses the next. Diaphanous gypsy blouses and tunics became the sartorial equivalent of anti-war posters. The outrageous flare of bell-bottom jeans had its own pedestal when women paired their hippie denim with two-to-four-inch platform shoes.

Glam rock and then punk, both imported from the U.K., ushered in first dandyish preferences for feather boas and lamé and then a uniform of leather and plaid. Disco also hustled its way into fashion, bringing jumpsuits, wrap dresses, tube tops, and hot pants. Man-made fibers like polyester, Lycra, and Lurex invaded.

The standout: 1970s
AN ETHNIC PEASANT DRESS

An ethnic peasant dress, with Renaissance sleeves and a flounce at the hem. I love the dreamy, bohemian feel of these ultrafemme frocks. You look like a woman who can bake a loaf of bread and trek across the desert on a camel. When Yves Saint-Laurent debuted his artisto-gypsy collection in 1976, the haute hippie was born and she still sashays down the current runways.

Because garish polyester prevailed throughout much of the decade, a silk or cotton peasant dress makes the perfect pick. You can choose from the styles that lace up at the bodice or gather at the waist in midcalf or maxi length. I'm a fan of the ones with ruffled scoop necklines, too. Dresses that feature Liberty prints—typically, small floral patterns—are my favorites because they evoke an innocent, girlish sensibility.

Wear it with: High-heeled knee-boots and oversized gold hoop earrings. A tailored jacket, buttoned halfway, injects some substance for contrast.

Other treasures to seek out: Floppy hats, belted leather jackets in rich colors like burgundy or forest green or patchwork design, and folk boho suede coats with embroidered Tyrolean borders.

1980<u>s</u>

"Super-Sized Glamour"

The style sensibility

Power dressing dominated the go-go eighties and women showed off their aerobics-taut physiques in spray-on silhouettes. Body-clinging dresses, leggings, bustiers, and catsuits made for maximum exposure. Corporate female dynamos, along with their assistants, postured in Claude Montana suits with giant shoulder pads.

The Christian Lacroix pouf skirt, which is one of my favorite looks from this era, spurred imitators and became must-have party wear. The brazen opulence of *Dynasty* drove women to wear blinding amounts of sequins and jumbo shrimp–sized jewels.

The standout: 1980s
ORNATE FITTED JACKETS

Ornate fitted jackets can become the focal point of any outfit. That celebration of excess and look-at-me mentality manifested itself in rich fabrics like brocade or jacquard. And because these garments are only twenty to thirty years old, you're likely to score styles in excellent condition.

I always look for smart fitted cuts with a subtle snake of peplum or layers upon layers of ruffles. You can find great leather bolero jackets in rainbow metallic colors, too. Just be mindful of voluminous arms that might make a piece look too costume-like. A tailor can easily take in the seams or remove shoulder pads, if need be.

Wear it with: A pair of leggings or stretch pants with a camisole and strappy sandals or stilettos. Try it with a little black dress for an evening look.

Other treasures to seek out: Strapless ruched velvet or taffeta cocktail dresses, pouf skirts, Gucci monogram bags, and wood and papier-mâché earrings.

A 1980s beaded evening bag masquerading as a 1920s accessory.

MODERN-DAY 1960S STYLE

People always ask me how to master that 1960s look. My advice is simple: Find the one vintage piece that works for you instead of wearing an early 1960s ensemble from head to toe. Vintage is a lot like drinking martinis. A little goes a long way. The trick is to incorporate that one sophisticated element into a modern outfit. You never want to look like you just walked off a Pan Am flight from 1962—unless, of course, you're en route to a *Mad Men* costume party.

Here are the most versatile and elegant staples that every woman owned back in the early 1960s. And each of these pieces can easily be worked into a contemporary outfit:

The sexy sheath	This body-skimming dress hugs the bust and hips and utterly adores an hourglass figure. (Don't forget the appropriate undergarments for a silk-smooth silhouette.)
Cigarette pants	Preferably in black, these flat-front, slim-cut pants that taper at the ankle are much more elegant and wearable than capris.
A shirtwaist dress	I practically consider this classic, tailored style with a nipped waist and full skirt to be a 1960s uniform.
A twin set	The classic combination of a cashmere shell and matching cardigan was an essential for daywear. I love them in camel and winter white.
A string of pearls	Jackie Kennedy often wore a luminous pearl necklace, and many women owned them in varying lengths and styles. Brooches, too, were an accessory staple for sweaters, jackets, and dresses.

A pearl and rhine-stone brooch from the estate of famed swing bandleader, Billy Eckstine.

Joan's secret weapon: *the pencil skirt*

The pencil skirt deserves its own love sonnet. Let me count the ways in which I adore it. It's classic, flirty, feminine, and so versatile. You can pair one with a tight sweater for the va-va-voom Joan Holloway look or tone down the come-hither effect with a ruffled blouse. For an ultramodern sensibility, add a bolero jacket or a simple tank top and a long strand of pearls.

Finding the perfect silhouette in a vintage pencil skirt is essential, but it could require dozens of trips to the dressing room. Take the piece to a trusted tailor instead and have it fitted precisely to your waist and hips. You can have it tapered as skinny at the hem as you dare.

Joan Holloway wears her pencil skirts hemmed at mid-knee, which flatters her. Experiment with lengths that range from midcalf to Joan's cut or even below the knee. You'll find the perfect fit for your sassy pencil skirt. Just make sure that the kick pleat is long enough. You want to wiggle, not hobble, your way across the room.

» *Take the piece to a trusted tailor instead and have it fitted precisely to your waist and hips. You can have it tapered as skinny at the hem as you dare.*

Banish secondhand flaws

Did you know that the word *vintage* originally comes from the Latin term *vindemia,* which means grape gathering? That suddenly makes a lot of sense when you unearth a great 1960s poncho emblazoned with a huge red-wine stain. In the world of vintage, certain flaws can be remedied. Others are deal breakers. Be sure to examine any item carefully and even hold it up in natural light to be certain that there is no fading at the shoulders. (Only 100 percent cotton garments can be dyed easily.)

Small moth holes in knits like sweaters can be darned with thread that matches the fabric. Garments with cigarette burns are trickier, especially silks, and require a patch job from the hem material that won't ever be seamless. Underarm perspiration stains are usually impossible to remove on delicate fabrics, but OxiClean or a paste of baking soda and water often works wonders on cottons and linens.

For perfume or body odor, I keep a spray bottle of vodka and water—a few spritzes will do the trick. (Yes, it seems like it's always cocktail hour on the set of *Mad Men.*) A rinse with white vinegar is the best remedy for the acrid scent of mothballs.

» *Modernist couture maestros like Paco Rabanne and André Courrèges top the coveted list of the vintage fashion cognoscenti.*

The vintage designers you should know

If you're label literate, you already know the big guns of vintage fashion like Emilio Pucci, Yves Saint Laurent, and Christian Dior. Seminal pieces by these designers typically get snapped up quickly by collectors and can fetch thousands of dollars at shops or auctions. (A pristine YSL Le Smoking couture tux can sell for upwards of $3,000.) Even lesser-known modernist couture maestros like Paco Rabanne and André Courrèges top the coveted list of the vintage fashion cognoscenti and can be difficult to find or afford.

Thankfully, a bevy of lesser-known names crafted amazing garments, too. One label I look for is Don Loper, a Beverly Hills costumer who created sexy lace party dresses and raw silk bolero jackets in the fifties and sixties. I use his pieces as inspiration for *Mad Men* looks. Lilli Ann, a San Francisco label

I adore, produced exquisite suits with velveteen cuffs and sumptuous shawl-collared tweed coats that you can buy online or at vintage shops.

Once you discover a designer you would like to collect, you can start trawling the Web or local vintage stores. (Do keep in mind, however, that many great pieces carry no label because they were hand-sewn by housewives.) Wanda Soileau, the owner of one of my favorite L.A. vintage boutiques, Playclothes (www.vintageplayclothes.com), knows enough about the subject to write a set of encyclopedias. So I asked her to name three of her favorite vintage designers and clue you in on which of their styles to seek out.

Emma Domb, a California-based dressmaker who designed from 1939 through the '70s and specialized in prom and party dresses. "Her earlier looks were more geared to the ingenue," says Soileau. "Later styles were more sexy and fitted."

Look for: Strapless cocktail dresses from the fifties with tapered waists and ballerina skirts. In the sixties Domb worked with fun vibrant colors and favored beaded bodices with chiffon skirts. *Expect to pay:* $75 to $350, depending upon the era.

Darlene, a popular manufacturer of silk-print floral sweaters during the 1950s and '60s. "You can tell a Darlene sweater right away because of the bright colors," Soileau says.

Look for: A floral cardigan with three-quarter or long sleeves in turquoise, yellow, or orange that fits at the waist. *Expect to pay:* $60 to $85.

Ceil Chapman, a New York designer who once partnered with Gloria Vanderbilt and created sexy cocktail dresses worn by Marilyn Monroe, Deborah Kerr, and Elizabeth Taylor. She designed a wedding dress for Jayne Mansfield.

Look for: Black taffeta dresses that feature exquisite draping, pin tucking, and boning above the waist. Her 1950s "wiggle" dresses are fit for modern-day pinups. *Expect to pay:* $200 to $600.

Vintage preservation

Taking care of vintage requires a few tricks of the trade and lots of TLC. My secret weapon for preserving vintage? Acid-free tissue paper, which has a neutral pH and will not transfer chemicals that could discolor or weaken fabrics. You can buy it in sheets or rolls. Wrap it around hangers to create a padding that will protect the fibers from stretching or tearing while they are hung. For heavily beaded pieces or delicate fabrics like chiffons, silks, organza, and lace, avoid hangers entirely. I always find that much of the wear and tear of a garment affects the shoulders. In fact, for that reason, museums like the Smithsonian store period costumes in acid-free cardboard boxes. You can opt for plastic bins—well lined with the acid-free paper—but remember to leave them unsealed so the pieces can breathe. (An excess of heat and moisture could cause colors to bleed or fabrics to swell.)

Ideally, the oldest and most delicate pieces should be laid out flat, which is not practical unless your closet rivals a hockey rink in square footage. Soft folding, akin to draping, with the acid-free tissue paper used as a buffer will prevent sharp creases that can split fibers. Remember to refold, using different creases, every six months to preserve those fibers. You can wad the tissue paper into a long tube shape and roll certain pieces as an alternative to folding.

Don't neglect those accessories. Hats, shoes, and handbags should always be stuffed, as well. That way they will maintain their shape. Exposure to sunlight is yet another damaging culprit, as fabrics can fade and become even more brittle from drying out. Be sure to store delicate vintage items in a cool, dark place. And a hug every now and then wouldn't hurt.

Beyond the wardrobe

For me, the allure of vintage extends well beyond dresses, shoes, hats, coats, and jewelry. My passion has become a part of my lifestyle. I love glamorous accoutrements from decades past, like Art Deco cigarette cases, which make sophisticated business card holders or ornaments for a coffee table.

My collection of vintage playing cards includes a 1950s deck from my grand-mother's bridge club, which is displayed on my bookshelf. I use them, too. Antique vanity sets, usually made up of a matching monogrammed brush, comb, and mirror, look so suave on a dresser top or bathroom counter. Vintage curios and furniture add depth and contrast to modern decor. Plus these trinkets make for fascinating visual tributes to the craftsmanship and culture of the past.

Cocktail CHATTER

THOUGH THE MINISKIRT HARKENS BACK TO THE SIXTIES THE SHORT STYLE DIDN'T TRULY TAKE OFF UNTIL 1966. Designer Mary Quant, who ran a boutique in London, popularized the mini, alongside French fashion maestro André Courrèges. Both vehemently claim credit for its invention. Courrèges once said of his revolutionary hemlines, "I wanted to make women liberated, full of life, modern. I think I achieved all that."

ACCORDING TO THE *NEW YORK TIMES,* Tokyo has the largest concentration of vintage shops, with over 400 boutiques. In 1966, the first store, called Chicago, opened to sell Levi's and flannel shirts to men seeking the casual, all-American look.

GOT A GUCCI HEIRLOOM IN YOUR FAMILY? Perhaps a chic iconic hobo bag or a logo travel satchel? Earlier this year, the design house teamed with Christie's auction house to offer an online appraisal service for its vintage luxury goods, called Gucci Collector. Simply upload photos of that Gucci gem and fill out a corresponding form to find out its value. (Go to Christies.com; process takes two to four weeks.)

CHECKLIST

Find your favorite fashion decade and then begin vintage shopping with a mission to collect its best offerings.

Do ask your mom if she—or any relative—collected costume jewelry or beaded clutches and might be interested in showing you her collection. Even if you can't borrow anything, you can always admire the handiwork.

Visit a vintage shop with a pair of jeans or a modern dress in hand to see how the retro pieces pair with your contemporary wardrobe. Remember to closely examine all pieces for tears or stains.

Invest in a vintage pencil skirt pronto and have it tailored to hug your waist and hips.

Take a moment to make sure that all of your delicate garments are stored properly in acid-free tissue paper. Accessories like handbags and hats should be stuffed with said paper, as well.

The
IMPORTANCE of being
ACCESSORIZED

Accessories are the surest cure-all for wardrobe ennui, not to mention the most economical way to overhaul your current inventory. And who hasn't peeked into her closet and rolled her eyes at the familiar dresses and jackets and skirts? Whenever I get a bit weary of my clothing roster, it's time to implement my surefire rejuvenation plan: Invest in a new accessory like a pair of glamorous oversized white sunglasses or a huge dramatic cocktail ring or some sleek cognac-hued riding boots.

Suddenly, older outfits feel fresh. A big, chunky necklace completely remodels a simple white tee. Exotic pumps—lizard or snakeskin or embossed leathers—make a pair of skinny jeans do an about-face. In other words, what a difference an accent can make. Even a new bright lip gloss, be it red or coral or peony pink, can alter the look of an outfit. In fact, you absolutely should introduce color into your wardrobe with accessories. It's the safest and easiest way to experiment with bold shades or fabrics on a more subtle scale. Shoes, handbags, and jewelry also allow you to try out a current trend without looking like a head-to-toe catwalk conformist.

But most importantly, certain accessories always get noticed. On *Mad Men*, I invest a sizable portion of the costume budget in jewelry. When the camera zooms in for Betty's tête-à-tête with Don, you see those flattering

I love to visually contrast Betty's prim femininity with Don's rugged machismo by designing costumes that heighten the juxtaposition. Her floral sheath and his cool, sharkskin suit also speak to the chasm in their relationship.

light-reflective pearls in her ears and at her throat. Ditto for the jet bead earrings that play off Joan's peaches-and-cream complexion.

When someone zeroes in on you, he or she typically views you from the shoulders up. So a scarf knotted at the neck or a peacock-feather hair comb become a central part of your close-up.

And you should *always* be ready for your close-up.

» A big, chunky necklace completely remodels a simple white tee. Exotic pumps—lizard or snakeskin or embossed leathers—make a pair of skinny jeans do an about-face. In other words, what a difference an accent can make.

An Erwin Pearl pearl, gold, and black leather necklace from the 1990s.

Seven variations on the little black dress

Like a freshly stretched blank canvas, the little black dress desperately seeks color and texture and definition. Its beauty lies in its utter devotion to your whims. Consider it a supplicant to your style and play Picasso.

The most shape-shifting of silhouettes would be the simple crepe wool or cotton sheath, preferably sleeveless. That design lends itself to untold translations with the addition of a few transformative accessories. So much so, in fact, that no one will even notice that your trusty frock has been out almost every night for the past week.

Here are seven ways to change up the look:

1 *Cinch it.* A leopard or zebra print belt, be it wide or skinny, will add both primal edge and stark contrast. Any punch of color, in fact, will define the waist and inject some splash. Try a belt in bright red, Kelly green, cobalt blue, or canary yellow.

2 *Re-create the outline.* A striking marabou bolero jacket in a pale pink or soft cream color not only re-creates the upper silhouette, it also becomes the highlight of your ensemble. A gold or silver sequined shrug has the same effect.

3 *Inject depth and flash.* A layered succession of different types of necklaces—pearls, gold chains, crystals, or jet beads— in varying lengths will create a sparkly bib that draws the admiring eye.

» *Like a freshly stretched blank canvas, the little black dress desperately seeks color and texture and definition.*

4 *Draw the eye upward.* **A** boater with a striped grosgrain ribbon at the brim or a small, jaunty cocktail hat can totally change the overall vibe of an outfit.

5 *Kick it up.* You can alternate between bare legs with nude heels for a more classic look and lace black or gray tights with fuchsia, white, or turquoise booties to exude a party-girl aura. For a saucy summer casual look, add an ethnic sandal like a strappy Mexican huarache and a vintage basket tote like a traditional straw-basket creel bag.

6 *Layer with accents.* A slouchy suede or fringed bag, worn satchel-style across the front, will create a new focal line. The accessory also adds a more bohemian slant to the look, which you can complement with a chunky necklace.

7 *Add padding.* In couture, the shoulders never get neglected. You can add some upper oomph to your dress with a band jacket that features structured shoulders. If your frock has sleeves, consider adding detachable shoulder pads to redefine the proportions.

More is more

Coco Chanel famously quipped about accessories: "Look in the mirror before you leave the house and take one thing off." With all due respect to the woman who innovated fashion, I must disagree. Perhaps back in her day, when ladies wore matching jewelry, gloves, hats, and scarves all at once, the impulse to overaccessorize called for a spot of temperance. But nowadays women don't rely on nearly as many accents to season an outfit.

For that reason, I say, "Wink at yourself in the mirror before you leave the house and add one more accessory." Maybe it's a gold-chain coin belt with eye-catching dangling currency. Or a trio of enamel bracelets in contrasting colors that clack gently when you make a point. On *Mad Men*, Pete Campbell's wife, Trudy, often wears two charm bracelets with a bangle and matching earrings and necklace.

Layering necklaces happens to be one of my signature styles. The more striking the better. I glean inspiration from the flamboyant beauty of accessory-worshipping African and Indian cultures. A Mumbai woman's bridal set includes an ornately colorful jeweled necklace with matching earrings and tikka, a pendant that sits on the forehead. Tribes in the Sudan adorn themselves in ivory bangles and neck rings, while the married women of Mali wear oversized gold crescent earrings. Such adornments offer more than mere decor. They tell a story or define a status. Let your accessories reveal a bit about you, too.

1990s stick pin by Agnes.

» *Wink at yourself in the mirror before you leave the house and add one more accessory.*

Christina Hendricks gave me this piece that I call my "punk rock bracelet."

Unexpected accomplices

A crystal spider shoulder brooch and a floral sequin appliqué that I use as a hair accessory.

It's too bad that hats, belts, and shoes can't transcend their utilitarian purposes. But thankfully, so many other accessories offer secondary and refreshingly uncommon uses. Case in point: A strand of pearls can be woven around an elastic band to secure a high ponytail stylishly, while a long chain doubles as a unique headband. (January Jones wore a long, delicate diamond necklace as a headband to the Emmys a few years ago and she seemed to hover above the red carpet with an angel's halo.) Last New Year's Eve, I added a flapper element to my formal look by bobby-pinning a crystal appliqué from a fabric store into my hair. Men, in particular, were smitten. Vintage clip-on earrings make perfect unusual accents for coifs, too. Pierced styles, like rhinestone flowers or even a simple pearl stud, can inject some panache into a lapel or a plain neckline.

Shoe clips, a fixture in the Victorian era, reinvigorate pumps and peep-toe platforms. You can find wonderful filigreed marcasite and pearl clips from the 1920s at vintage stores or browse modern sites like shoeworthy.com. Dress clips, typically worn on the straps, transform the look of a frock, and just one looks great on a belt or attached to a chain as a pendant. I also adore slender stick pins, which elegantly amp up a lapel or a scarf or even a T-shirt. My collection of stick pins includes a piece with oversized jewels on one end and others that feature dangling pearls and leaves dipped in gold. Vintage hair combs, too, are a favorite accessory staple of mine. Look for Art Deco–inspired designs from the 1920s or '30s festooned with crystals or seed pearls.

Scarves work overtime

You can tell a lot about a lady by the way she sports a scarf. The effect can be studied or carefree, artistic or as prim as a porcelain teacup. Glamour-puss Joan Holloway goes all out, wearing hers in a dramatic kerchief style, much like Sophia Loren. To try it, fold the scarf into a triangle shape and then crisscross the tails beneath the chin before knotting at the nape of the neck. Add oversized sunglasses and you're suddenly an Italian starlet hiding out in Capri. Campari, anyone? Betty Draper, on the other hand, downplays the theatrics by donning a silk printed scarf that's demurely knotted at her throat.

No other accessory works as hard as a scarf. It's an accent willing to bend to your every whim. You can wear one, depending on its dimensions, around the neck in a jaunty bow or as a vibrant belt with jeans. Experiment with it to create a preppy headband or a gypsy-style head scarf. With an oversized version, like the thirty-six-inch-square Hermès scarf, you can make a sexy triangular top that ties in back, or a bandeau.

When I was fifteen I found my most prized scarf, with a tiger motif and jungle print, at the Galeries Lafayette in Paris. It's still in heavy rotation. Now my collection consists of hundreds of scarves in all shapes and sizes, ranging from a small printed silk handkerchief that is worn as a pocket square to an oversized scarf that doubles as a sarong. Forage through those baskets of scarves at vintage shops and thrift stores to start your own collection.

Barton Perreira ivory shell "Temptress" sunglasses with smoky topaz lens.

A bouquet of designer scarves, including my very first Hermès.

» No other accessory works as hard as a scarf.
It's an accent willing to bend to your every whim.

The principles of highly effective purses

With the advent of the luxury designer "it" bags a few years ago, collecting expensive handbags became a competitive sport among women. I'm so glad that trend is now as passé as the bare midriff. For me, purses hold incredible allure because they easily revitalize an outfit. A sleek and shiny taupe snakeskin clutch imbues an opulent edge to a casual look, while an oversized red suede tote adds some attitude to a black business suit. And because purses come in a plethora of shapes, sizes, and different leathers, you can truly express your individuality by what you carry.

My personal collection of handbags spans decades, dating back to an 1860s cranberry velvet coin purse. Timeless day bags like the crescent-shaped hobos and chain-strap shoulder styles never skitter out of fashion, so you can wisely invest in one and know that you'll carry it for twenty or even thirty years. I always keep three different styles of handbags at my office. Inside my huge Jil Sander suede work tote that carries scripts and my computer and notebooks I also stash a couple of clutches for a day-to-night quick change. (By all means, store an extra dressy purse—in its dustbag—in your trunk or at the office for last-minute dinner party invitations.)

On *Mad Men*, both Betty and Joan match their bags to their shoes, a fashion habit for many women back in the 1960s. Betty owns a variety of lizard-skin, alligator, and crocodile pumps in brown, black, and cream, each with a coordinating frame purse. Joan's pocketbook choices are more colorful, since she tends to match her bag to her shoes *and* her jewel-toned dresses. That custom no longer holds, and you needn't perfectly harmonize all your accessories. (Though matching a shoe to a purse, on occasion, appears wonderfully classic and ladylike.)

Here are the four basic handbag styles that every woman should have on hand:

1 *An oversized leather tote* for the workplace. Designers know that women need chic briefcases and so most styles can handle a computer, files, and a pound or two of cosmetics. Look for polished hardware like gold closures or metal embellishments, which look professional.

» Because purses come in a plethora of shapes, sizes, and different leathers, you can truly express your individuality by what you carry.

2 A *tailored day bag* in black, beige, or white with simple, elegant lines. Equestrian-inspired purses—think Gucci, Coach, and Mulberry—are as classic and versatile as a cardigan.

3 *The all-purpose clutch,* be it a fold-over, envelope, or round pochette, complements almost any look for late day or night. Don't shy away from bright colors or patent leather or even embellishments like studs or grommets.

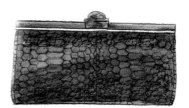

4 An *evening bag* is essential for formal events. Rather than fret over precise color combinations, you can always pick up a metallic silk, leather, or skin—in gold, silver, copper, or bronze—that works with any gown.

That wiggle

You probably have a love-hate relationship with your high heels. Who hasn't had a one-night stand with a pair of stilettos that brutalized her toes? Or cursed the ankle pinch of a brand-new sling-back? Whine all you want. As a Southern girl, I absolutely insist on them. Insist. Just be sure to have your foot measured at a shoe store, as the proper sizing will increase the comfort. High heels make a huge difference. They force you to stand up straighter and lengthen your silhouette. Your buttocks protrude 22 percent more, thanks to the boost.

Without those three-inch pumps, Joan Holloway would have a lot less wiggle. That sexy swagger, her hips swaying like a hypnotic pendulum, comes mostly because of her three-inch heels. In fact, the actress Christina Hendricks, who plays Joan, always says to me, "The higher the better" when I dress her for a scene. She also secretly admits that wearing heels is no picnic, but she's willing to endure the sacrifice for the sex appeal.

To learn how to glide effortlessly, or even trot, if necessary, try this traditional charm-school method: Walk back and forth in heels with a few books atop your head. (If you're too skittish on stilettos or new to heels, you can opt for wedges, which provide height and stability. Or look for platform heels, which build in height at the toe and subsequently offer a more balanced lift.) And by always keeping your thumbs facing forward, you can be sure that your shoulders are elegantly thrown back. It makes your clothes look so much better. The Sterling Cooper secretaries get an earful whenever they shuffle. "Hold those shoulders back," I plead.

Hello, customs agent

As an aspiring jet-setter determined to circle the globe, I have never left a country or an island without a special native trinket stashed in my luggage. I love to shop African bazaars, French flea markets, and any little out-of-the-way shops or stands that offer locally made artifacts. Most of my most prized accessories, in fact, come from my travels. In Morocco, I found an oversized sterling silver and poppy-red coral bead necklace that never fails to add pow to any outfit. A recent trip to Panama introduced me to the amazing hand-loomed wool textiles of the region. I brought home a tablecloth in rich, dramatic stripes and geometric motif, which has become a favorite shawl. In Tortola, I nabbed a pair of 14 karat gold hibiscus earrings.

Next time you travel, be sure to venture to the local marketplace. You can even do some research beforehand to find out the specialty item of the region. In Colombia, high-quality emeralds sell at fantastic rates. Delicately carved coral cameo rings, brooches, and pendants sell along the major canals in Venice, along with gorgeous handmade lace. The hand-woven tie-dyed Matmi silk that sells in Bangkok can be cut and sewn into trousers or suits by a tailor.

Upon touching down in a new place, I quickly seek out the center for the marketplace or ask the hotel concierge for some shopping tips. At the very least, you can always carry home a coin and have a jeweler make it into a pendant for a necklace or bracelet. My father collected coins and had many of his most cherished pieces made into rings and pendants. Exotic souvenirs not only serve as fantastic reminders of a trip, but they also trigger stimulating conversations about future travels.

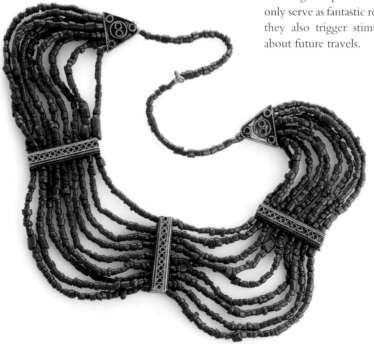

Imagine being overlooked in this saucy 1940s hat, adorned with fruit and tulle? Never.

A weakness for hats

Emily Post once said, "It is impossible for a hatless woman to be chic." That was her take back in 1959, and up until the late sixties many women agreed. A half-century later, I half agree. Or, rather, let me say that a woman in a hat is usually twice as chic. There are specific rules about when a man can wear a hat, but a woman has carte blanche—though donning a chapeau in an office isn't advised unless you work for a fashion magazine or a milliner. My own vast collection of chapeaus includes berets, fedoras, and floppy hats à la Ali MacGraw. I have a red straw hat with a polka-dotted veil from the eighties that makes me smile before I even put it on. To get a sense of the impact of a hat, think of Faye Dunaway in *The Thomas Crown Affair* peeking out from beneath the tilted brim of her fedora.

In my experience, many women become as skittish as spooked horses around my favorite accessory. Their eyes widen and they shake their heads and say, "I don't look good in hats." That is, until they exhale and fiddle with the brim or shape and see how utterly darling a cloche or Breton can be. The key to finding the right color and size is to try on as many as possible. (Vintage stores typically carry a huge supply, as do many upscale department stores like Saks and Neiman Marcus.) A more low-key hat like a fedora or boater works best with relaxed outfits like pantsuits and sundresses, while cocktail hats commandeer dressier, tailored looks.

*"Panama" straw
fedora with embroi-
dered spider.*

*The plaid Italian
wool "Elmer Cap"
with pom-pom.*

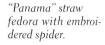

*Fur velour "Fierce
Fedora" with origami
grosgrain trim.*

» *A woman in a hat is usually twice as chic. The key to finding
the right color and size is to try on as many as possible.*

*"Flower Pot" sun hat
with feather print.*

All hats by Tracy Watts

» There are so many new products that make it simple to "dress up" your face in minutes.

Lips & lashes: *the final touches*

If the leading ladies of *Mad Men* ever appeared onscreen without their signature makeup, the wow factor would surely fizzle. Their matte crimson pouts and dramatically lined eyes are as much a part of their characters as the pencil skirts and stilettos. Credit makeup department head Lana Horchowski, who, along with her amazing team, can transform as many as eighty faces for an episode. "Women were supposed to be beautiful all the time for their husbands," she says of the quintessential 1960s housewife. "They had one basic look back then: fresh and simple."

For that sixties face, Horchowski relies on MAC's Virgin Isle Cream Colour Base on the cheeks for a soft blush of coral. (Powder blushes didn't hit the cosmetics market until 1963. Same goes for shimmer products and glosses.) She also fills in lips with Clinique's Hint of Pink liner or NARS Barbarella lipstick; a sweep of mascara with a thin swath of MAC Fluidline eyeliner on the upper lash line completes her look. For evenings, those lash lines thicken in size and a bright lipstick like MAC's Vegas Volt accelerates the look. False eyelashes add further amplification.

Blessedly, women—and makeup—have come a long way since those days of basting roasts and keeping house. And there are so many new products that make it simple to "dress up" your face in minutes. I asked Horchowski to put together a simple and quick regimen for creating a modern-day look.

Here are five basic elements for looking polished:

1 A *light tinted moisturizer* with SPF to even out the skin tone. (Use a spot concealer under the eyes, if necessary.)

2 A *swath of peach or coral blush,* which best mimics a natural healthy flush. These neutral shades work for any complexion.

3 *Use mascara* and be sure to stroke those tiny inner and longer outer lashes for a full and balanced effect.

4 A *neutral lip gloss* that adds subtle color and shimmer to your pout. Look for a shade that is a little brighter than your natural lip hue. Rosy pinks and peachy browns are the most versatile, subtle tones.

5 *Finally, fill in your eyebrows* with a pencil or powder to define the shape. These arches are the focus of all of your expressions and get more notice than you might think. If you're having trouble finding colors online, please consult your local cosmetics counter.

When I was growing up, my mother would tell me the story of how my grandmother, Etoile Lillard Chesnutt, always nagged her about her bare pout. "Dottie, would you please just put on the lipstick?" she would plead. (Mom was more interested in horses than glamour.) I, on the other hand, became obsessed with makeup at a very early age and favored foundation and purple and teal eye shadows. Nowadays I always wear lip gloss and mascara—even to play tennis. But my all-time favorite beauty ritual calls for tweezers, glue, and a steady hand. False eyelashes are my beauty obsession because nothing beats that come-hither flutter and to secure it and flatten any air pockets. To achieve that sexy cat eye, apply more lashes to the upper and outer corner.

Don't fear the smoky eye either, which is actually easier to execute than it appears. The key to avoiding that raccoon in the headlights look is to opt for softer tones like dark brown and slate gray instead of stark black.

Many companies offer palettes that instruct on where to apply each specific color. Maybelline's Expert Wear Eye Shadow Quad in Charcoal Smokes includes a family of colors that make for the perfect smoky eye.

> *» Growing up, my mother would tell me the story of how my grandmother, Etoile Lillard Chesnutt, always nagged her about her bare pout.*

you can experiment with different lengths and styles. Add a few faux bottom lashes for the 1960s Twiggy effect or do a heavy, dark fringe of lash to create edgy impact for a rock-and-roll look.

If you're unseasoned in the fine art of false-lash application, it's easiest to work with lash strips. Horchowski recommends that you snip strips into minisegments rather than wrestle with the flimsy individual lashes, which can be tricky for first-timers. Apply a dot of the adhesive to the strip or section and to your upper lash line, then let both dry. (Even dry, they will adhere.) That way you have less mess and more control when you position the lashes with a tweezer. Don't forget to tamp down the actual strip

Follow these four steps to create the perfect smoky eye:

1   *Apply a primer* or foundation to the lid so that the shadow will endure.

2   *Brush your lighter gray* or brown shadow onto the entire lid and then add a slightly darker shade to the inner and outer corners of the lid.

3   *Draw a line along* the upper lash line and then highlight the lower lash line with either a gel liner or even the darker eye shadow and a sharp brush.

4   *Now, smudge and blend* with a soft brush to get rid of any harsh lines.

» *Don't fear the smoky eye either, which is actually easier to execute than it appears.*

On to that perfect *siren-worthy red lip*, aka the Holy Grail of beauty for most women. (A crimson pout is always bold and appropriate, if you wear it with confidence. Some women wake up and put on their lips before they sip that first cup of coffee.) To prevent the color from bleeding, line the lips with a neutral light pink or nude pencil. Horchowski favors NARS Velvet Matte Lip Pencil in Dragon Girl, an upbeat red with blue undertones, because it flatters most skin tones. She also likes DuWop's new Private Red, a rich, creamy lipstick that adjusts its crimson hue to suit your own lip color. Her on-set secret for achieving a pout with staying power? She applies the color and then adds a light dusting of powder before applying another coat. One last note: Pick one feature to highlight and employ a subtle hand with your other assets. If you opt for a red lip, avoid dramatic eye makeup and vice versa.

» A crimson pout is always bold and appropriate, if you wear it with confidence. Some women wake up and put on their lips before they sip that first cup of coffee.

MY FAVORITE BEAUTY PICKS

Behind every woman are a few good beauty products, right? Here are my must-have paints and potions:

NOW Grapeseed Oil: Grapeseed oil contains a high amount of antioxidants and anti-aging properties. I apply this amazing light oil all over my body every day, after I shower. And I use it as a moisturizer on my face and neck.	**Amour Lip Gloss:** My favorite shades are the plummy opaque Last Dance and Kashmir, a shimmery pink. These glosses go on smooth and the color lasts for hours.
Benefit Smokin' Eyes: I love this palette because it explains, step-by-step, how to get that perfect, smoldering smoky eye. I always carry it in my makeup bag.	**Napoleon Perdis Prismatic Eyeshadow Quad #12:** All four colors—pearly white, soft pink, and a light and dark shimmery taupe—blend perfectly for a natural day or night eye.
Maybelline Falsies Mascara: My lashes always look the longest and thickest with this fantastic mascara. Plus, it's affordable and doesn't irritate my eyes.	**Topstick Fashion-Fix Body Tape:** A red carpet staple! It's great for keeping those low-cut dresses, straps, and slippery fabrics in place.
Dr. Bronner's Magic Soaps: The peppermint always wakes me up in the morning. I love the zing!	**Benefit Erase Paste:** I appreciate the creamy consistency of this concealer and cover-up. It never lets me down.
Anastasia Brow Pen: It has a fine tip for application, stays on forever and gives a natural look to an enhanced arch.	**Nailtini Nail Polish:** Caviar Cocktail, Navy Grog, and Amaretto Fizz are my favorite colors. These polishes are free of formaldehyde, toluene, and DBP. Their Dry Martini Nail Polish Drying Spray works presto-quick and smells great, too.

Now, you're accessorized from head to lips to toe.

Cocktail CHATTER

THE COCKTAIL RING, that flashy signifier of good times and endless pours, first appeared during Prohibition in the 1920s. Flappers donned these immense baubles when attending gin joints and jazz clubs that served illicit alcoholic concoctions.

IN THE 1950S, the very first stilettos featured a metal tip on the base of the spiked heel that scratched and chipped floors. Hence, the sexy yet lethal shoe was banned from certain museums and buildings.

THANK COCO CHANEL for that chic wardrobe staple, the "little black dress." Her sleek simple style debuted in 1926 and *Vogue* promptly deemed it: "The frock that all the world will wear." Indeed, a deluge of LBDs soon followed.

CHECKLIST

Devote an hour or so to varying the look of your little black dress with accessories like belts, wraps, and bangles or gloves.

Add one high-impact accessory, be it a bold necklace or an oversized vintage brooch, to your ensemble just before you leave the house.

Get intimate with a splashy silk scarf by experimenting with its myriad uses. Try it on as a belt, kerchief style, or even as a gypsy headband.

Take an inventory of your handbag collection and determine if any need some professional TLC like cleaning or restitching or new handles. Many shoe-repair specialists also work with purses.

On a quiet night, perfect your application of a sixties-style smoky eye or sultry red pout or false eyelashes for the next cocktail party.

The
DON DRAPER
MAKEOVER

7

While women's fashion flits from fad to fad like a honeybee, menswear stands by and has a good chuckle. In fact, it's that deference to time-honored tradition and protocol that makes me adore clothing and accessories for men. The classics, from navy blue blazers to Irish-knit sweaters, never lose an iota of appeal. Sure, suit styles shift over the years. But the fundamentals of two basic pieces remain the same. How refreshing.

My own obsession with menswear didn't truly ignite until I started my career as a costume designer for films and television. While costuming the series *Deadwood*, which was set in South Dakota in the 1870s, I designed wardrobes for a whole town of men and became obsessed with jacket lengths and the different textures of wools, brocades, and velvets. One of the characters, legendary lawman Wild Bill Hickok, had flamboyant taste in apparel. For him I designed a cape lined with vivid plaid and a gold-and-black-houndstooth waistcoat and trousers piped in gold with an embroidered back. He also wore a big black hat with a large brim. Now that was a man who knew how to cut a figure.

Like Wild Bill, men should have fun with their style and fan those peacock feathers on occasion. There are so many different ways to show personality through fashion. During the 1970s, my own father, Paul Edwin Bryant II, favored a splashy wool-and-cashmere-blend plaid suit with oversized lapels and flared trousers. And speaking of memorable men, scores of esteemed gents, from Beau Brummell to Sherlock Holmes, expressed themselves through their style. And guess what? Tough guys do wear velvet.

Man meets suit

A good man in a great suit can be hard to find. When I first started fitting Jon Hamm as Don Draper, I had him try on many different suits before I discovered the right match in cut and silhouette. Once I found it, that transformation from modern-day actor to enigmatic 1960s ad exec was complete. Not only did he access his character through the suit, but he also admired his new look. "Wow! I love the way I look," he told me. His slim-cut jackets feature narrow lapels and collars with diagonal pockets, which are very flattering to any male silhouette.

Now, I'm not suggesting that a man spend all afternoon trying on trousers and jackets. But a well-cut, smartly fitted suit creates such an elegant line. Talk about poise and power. It's like style dynamite. One can start the quest for that suit by shopping off the rack, but know that all suits require a nip here or a hem there. Plus, many men assume they're one size bigger than their actual proper fit. That's probably because in a modern-day world, men have been schooled to seek out comfort over fit. My suggestion is that he first try on one size down—meaning if he thinks he's a 42, go with the 40. At the very least, it will be a good comparison exercise. To measure a man's chest, have him raise his arms slightly and relax his stomach. Snake the tape high around the chest and be sure to circle completely across the shoulder blades.

Now let's cover the basics. It's most important that the jacket fit in the shoulders. I like to see the shoulder seam line up perpendicular to the fall of the arm. As for the hem of the jacket, I have a tried-and-true rule. A man should stand with his arms at his sides in the jacket and curl up his hands, with his fingers against his thighs. The hem should rest in the crease of the palm naturally. If it bunches up, the jacket is too long and will look like his father's suit. If the hem falls above that crease, it's too short. (Unless he's going for that mod, exaggerated prep-school look.)

With trousers, it's all about fit, too. Mind any puddling at the ankle, as it renders the silhouette sloppy. A shorter "break," where the pant leg meets the shoes, or no break at all elongates the line. A man on a limited budget should always cash in on the versatility that comes with a charcoal, black, or navy suit.

» A well-cut, smartly fitted suit creates such an elegant line. Talk about poise and power. It's like style dynamite.

Is that a French accent?

Nothing makes me giddier than the glint of a monogrammed gold cuff link. It's a small detail that elevates a man's style from that of John Doe to James Bond. For far too long, men have relied on ties as their sole adornment. How sad. If only they knew that a bevy of accessories awaits them.

Don Draper always wears shirts with French cuffs, and he has an assortment of cuff links, ranging from bold gold and silver geometrics to a droll pair of crossed golf clubs set in mother-of-pearl. I typically avoid rounded ones for him because rectangles and squares better reflect his austerity and edge. Some of his cuff links are accented with stones, like lapis, which add a punch of color to the sleeve. (Knotted-silk-cord cuff links are a great, inexpensive alternative.)

Don also favors monogrammed belt buckles, which always match the metal of his cuff links. Be sure to pair gold with gold and silver with its own.

Roger Sterling may not wear his heart on his sleeve, but you'll always spot his initials. All of his barrel-cuff shirts feature a block monogram, which is the ultimate nod to sophistication. He also sports tie tacks and collar bars in silver. Quick primer: Tie tacks are, in essence, pins that secure the tie through a shirt button. A collar bar, fitted behind the knot of the tie, tames the collar and gently nudges the knot a bit upwards.

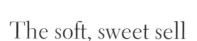

An array of snazzy tie tacks.

The soft, sweet sell

» *If your man refuses to shop at all, you might consider taking his measurements and playing personal stylist.*

Some men bristle when it comes to fashion. They might balk at the finery of French cuffs or the slim silhouette of an Italian suit. In essence, it's usually just a fear of the unknown. It's my job, as a costume designer, to assure the actors that the clothes are appropriate and will indeed make the character. When Jon Hamm first saw the high-rise suit pants he would wear as Don

Draper, he exclaimed, "That's the longest zipper I have ever seen!" Without missing a beat, I responded, "Don't you just love these long zips? Welcome to the sixties."

If you're trying to convince a dubious husband, friend, son, or brother to try on a look, I suggest you employ my technique. Tickle the ego before you pass along the piece in question by telling him that this tweed vest or that velvet smoking jacket suits his daring persona. You want to generate some pep and enthusiasm before he even starts disrobing.

If your man refuses to shop at all, you might consider taking his measurements and playing personal stylist. You can bring home a few fresh looks and ply him with a glass of single-malt scotch as he models clothes in the comfort of his own abode. Put on a Frank Sinatra CD to add macho ambience. In short, make it feel more like recreational fun than a chore.

HONOR THY TAILOR

Even the best suits cry out for alterations, so a man should get to know a trusted tailor. Pants will be shortened and jackets may call for a nip or tuck.

Here's a quick peek at his weapons of choice:

Shears for cutting patterns and/or trimming fabric.

A tape measure, which will gauge the chest, waist, sleeves, and neck size, along with the inseam.

Chalk to note the precise adjustments directly on the fabric.

White cotton thread or basting stitches, which will later be replaced with the appropriate silk thread.

A thimble for pushing that needle through the heavier fabrics.

His ten wardrobe essentials

The following basic wardrobe must-haves add up to an infinite number of outfits. Just glancing at the list, a few simple style equations come to mind like a dress shirt paired with jeans or a knit polo with a khaki summer suit. (Casual staples like shorts and sneakers and swim trunks are not included.)

1 *An overcoat:* Depending upon the climate, a neutral overcoat in fine-quality wool or a trench coat is fundamental to a complete look with a suit. The classic length falls above the knee, but longer versions can be found. A trench with detachable linings that zip in and out is the most versatile outerwear.

2 *Two suits:* A smart tailored suit, much like a uniform, never wavers from its intention to make a man look better. For colder months, a gray suit is always on the mark. (A black suit can look severe during the day.) A cotton or linen summer suit in khaki, off white, or even seersucker can be dressed down with flip-flops and a tee.

3 *One sports jacket:* Less constructed and formal than a suit jacket, the blazer adds polish to any casual look and can be made of any fabric, from cashmere to corduroy. Here's an opportunity to experiment with pattern options like tweed or tartan or herringbone.

» *The blazer adds polish to any casual look and can be made of any fabric, from cashmere to corduroy.*

4   *Three dress shirts:* Though color and pattern choices abound, two white button-front shirts and a light blue one will always work with almost all of the above. Be mindful of the condition of collars and cuffs, which wear out first.

5   *A silk tie:* The classic rep tie, a diagonally striped tie that originated in Britain and signified a man's private school or club, is the most versatile and striking of designs—if you must own just one. Other choices include solids and patterns that speak to you.

6   *Three casual shirts:* A couple of sporty knit polo shirts and well-fitted T-shirts are indispensable items for dressing down without sacrificing good style.

7   *One sweater:* As dependable as a pocketknife, the classic crew or V-neck pullover can class up any combination of separates.

8   *Two pairs of trousers:* A pair of black dress slacks, preferably in a light wool for longevity, and casual pants like khakis or cords round out the trouser arsenal of denim and suit pants. Both mate well with sweaters, sports jackets, and polos.

9   *Three pairs of shoes:* A suit has needs, like the right shoes. A pair of lace-up black oxfords is always appropriate, and a slip-on, be it a loafer or a driving moccasin, in brown makes the perfect alternative for jeans and more sporty looks. Suede desert boots or hip Chelsea boots make useful additions, too.

10   *A tuxedo:* Though it may sound extraneous, a tuxedo will be essential attire for every man at some point in his life. Buy one in early January, when most formal wear goes on sale, to avoid the dreaded and costly rental.

CLASSIC FABRICS FOR MEN'S CLOTHES

1. gray and black herringbone 2. brown and tan herringbone 3. gray and blue glen plaid 4. worsted flannel 5. camel-colored herringbone 6. houndstooth 7. black herringbone 8. navy plain weave

» A smart tailored suit, much like a uniform, never wavers from its intention to make a man look better.

I designed this sleek, slim-cut suit, known as the Mad Men edition, for Brooks Brothers.

Color wheels & character

How to distinguish a leading man in a sea of suits? As I mentioned early on in Chapter 1, color is my shorthand for creating a character. On *Mad Men*, in particular, the cast of gents spends most of their time in a buttoned-up Madison Avenue office. Just imagine trying to discern their individual personas if each one donned a gray flannel suit with a white shirt and blue-striped tie.

To keep these characters visually asunder, each man owns his color palette. While Don Draper rarely strays from a vast family of grays, Pete Campbell advertises his heady aspirations in charismatic shades of teal and French blue. Roger Sterling opts more for navy and black, while Sal Romano gets to bask in opulent shades of burgundy, gold, and green. Of course each guy has his own unique taste in ties, too.

A man should absolutely experiment with color to find the hue that suits his complexion and disposition.

Typically, *fair-skinned* chaps look best in subtle shades like blues, browns, and beiges. (Florid tones like maroon and orange can wash out the features.)

Medium-complected men can sample from the gamut, but should avoid olives or tans that precisely match their skin.

Finally, men with a *dark complexion* should opt for contrast in color and seek out light blues and soft grays or browns. (Severe shades like black and deep brown should be avoided if the palette closely matches the skin.)

A jaunty stingy brim fedora with a grosgrain ribbon band.

HAT SIZES

Stylish men from Frank Sinatra to Johnny Depp favor hats because they add instant élan. Boaters, fedoras, and even ball caps should always fit properly, though. (Measure the circumference of the head at the center of the forehead.) Most importantly, a man should understand that a hat is never worn inside.

Head Size	Hat Sizes	
21"	6 5/8	XS
21 1/2"	6 3/4	S
21 3/4"	6 7/8	
22"	7	M
22 1/2"	7 1/8	
22 3/4"	7 1/4	L
23"	7 3/8	
23 1/2"	7 1/2	XL
24"	7 5/8	
24 3/8"	7 3/4	XXL
24 7/8"	7 7/8	
25 1/8"	8	XXXL
25 1/2"	8 1/8	

A rainbow of Brooks Brothers shirts and ties.

Anatomy of a dress shirt

A sudden gust of wind should not disrupt a man's silhouette. His dress shirt never billows in the chest or out the back—unless he's a pirate. Fit is always key, from the collar to the cuffs. Anyone who has sauntered into my dressing room knows all about my take on the "two-finger rule." When a man tries on a dress shirt, I gauge the fit of the collar by testing the gap in the neckline. If I can insert two fingers, it's time to go down a half-size. (Many guides allow for two digits, but I find that a tie puckers if the collar has too much give.) The forefinger fit is optimum for achieving a sleek profile. For the proper size, circle a tape measure around the neck and across the Adam's apple. The shirt neck size will be a half-inch more than the measurements of the actual neck.

To ascertain sleeve length, the measurements must be taken from the middle of the upper back to across the shoulder and then continue down the back of the arm to the wrist bone. The cuff will cover the wrist and graze the root of the thumb; when worn with a blazer, a half-inch of the cuff should peek out. (That extension of the cuff elongates the arms, by the way.) Note that the tips of the shirt collar must always rest on the breast of the shirt and not rear like a wild mustang when a man swivels his neck. There are also different prescribed silhouettes for dress shirts, like the regular fit, slim fit, and athletic cut. A regular fit offers the fullest cut, while the slim fit will be narrower in chest and waist. The athletic version features a broad cut in the chest that tapers in the waist.

On to the aesthetics. A man can playfully assert himself through his dress shirts in so many different ways. In addition to myriad color options, there are patterns like stripes, gingham, houndstooth, herringbone twill, and ribbed twill, which lends a gentle sheen to the shirt. When it comes to cuffs, options include the traditional barrel style with buttons or the more formal French version, which is worn folded back and secured with cuff links.

Last, men should know that a wealth of collar shapes awaits—from the straight to the tab to the button-down.

» *A man can playfully assert himself through his dress shirts in so many different ways.*

The straight, being the most basic collar with up to a three-inch gap between the points, can be worn with or without a tie.

The spread collar, clocking in over that three inches, adds a bit more European flair.

Introduced by Brooks Brothers in 1896, *the button-down* is actually the most casual of collars and didn't appear on dress shirts until the 1950s. But my all time favorite collars are the more sophisticated tab and club styles. The tab, first worn by the Prince of Wales, features a small strap at the throat, which emphasizes the necktie knot by gently thrusting it forward.

The club collar, worn by Elvis and Mick Jagger, stands out for its rounded edges.

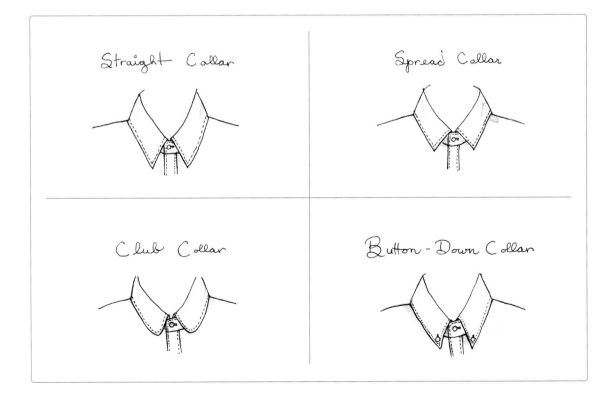

Straight Collar

Spread Collar

Club Collar

Button - Down Collar

The Tao of ties

If diamonds are a girl's best friend, then neckwear is certainly a gentleman's good chum. The right tie, be it a splashy paisley cravat or a scholarly rep style in a Windsor knot, can be as declarative as an engraved business card. If you're intuitive, you might even be able to divine a man's personality, position, and politics by his tie. As for length, the modern tie should fall at about midbelt and no lower. A shorter tie harkens to a period look.

There are four distinct knots and each one adds its own character to an ensemble.

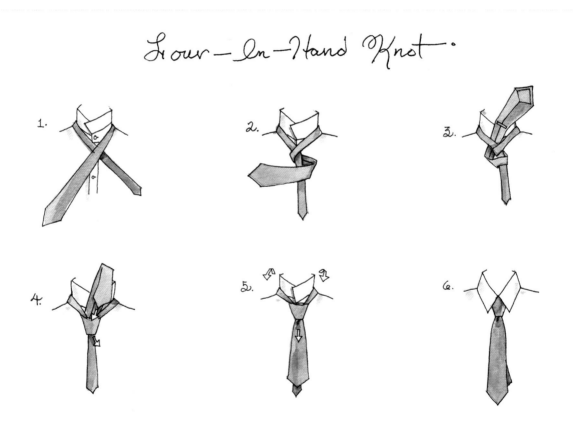

The Four-in-Hand: Named for the manner in which British carriage drivers tied their neckwear, this simple and popular knot is the most narrow and understated style. Perfect for button-down or spread collars.

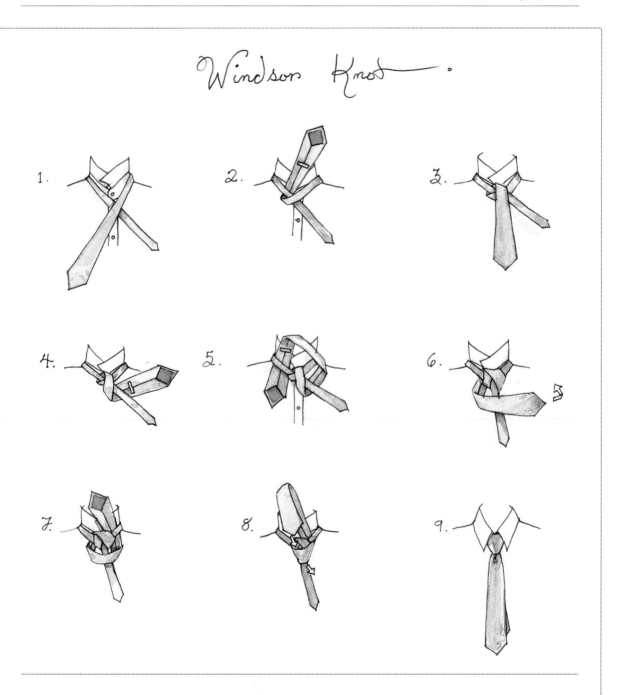

Windsor Knot ⎯ .

1.

2.

3.

4.

5.

6.

7.

8.

9.

The Windsor: More formal than the four-in-hand, this wide, triangular knot exudes clout and confidence. Be sure to pair it with a cutaway-collared dress shirt that can accommodate the thicker knot.

Bow Tie

1.

2.

3.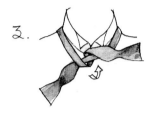

4.

5.

6.

7.

8.

The Bow Tie: Though often reserved for black-tie events, the sprightly bow tie has made a comeback as a day-to-day accent among the hip, young, and restless. I approve. To master the knot, a man can practice on his thigh. And know that all of the principal actors on *Mad Men* can turn out a bow tie.

1.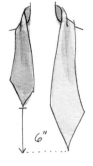

6"

2.

3.

4.

5.

6.

The Ascot or the Cravat: Historically beloved by Hollywood directors and randy millionaires, this always-pure-silk tie can be worn formally or with irony. Patterns include paisley, foulard, and polka dots.

Socks: *a love story*

Socks are often as neglected as orphans when it comes to style. But these simple utilitarian accessories do impact the overall effect of an outfit. In fact, I have a personal affinity for them. During the Depression, my grandfather, William Porter Chesnutt, founded Niota Textile Mills, where they manufactured socks. My idyllic childhood included many an afternoon spent at the sock mill, watching a giant machine flip socks right side out after adding seams. Believe it or not, this process intrigued me for hours on end.

History aside, I value socks for their ability to inject a flash of flair. A pair of red socks with a dark suit à la Fred Astaire says "fashion rebel"—though those shoes had better be up to snuff. Navy or forest green socks work well with a khaki suit, too. In the movie *Guys and Dolls*, there is a scene where all of the guys are wearing brightly colored socks with their pinstripes and tweeds while they dance in the boiler room.

As for matching socks to a suit, opinions clash. On *Mad Men*, I coordinate the socks to the trousers. It suits the characters on the show to abide by this sartorial tradition. (Just be sure to pick a sock that falls within the range of the shade without being the exact hue.) But selecting socks that pick up a color in a tie or dress shirt is also perfectly acceptable—even a bit more original.

» *I value socks for their ability to inject a flash of flair.*

From here to formality

Allow me to lament the decline of black tie for just a moment. Back in the day, such a dress code called for a proper tuxedo coat with formal trousers, pleated front shirt with studs and cuff links, a bow tie, and patent-leather shoes. A smart white dinner jacket could replace a tuxedo coat, but only if the event fell between Memorial and Labor Days. For other seasons there are plenty of options, from velvet to brocade dinner jackets. Incidentally, white tie, which has practically gone the way of the dodo, calls for a tailcoat with a white pique bow tie and matching vest. A morning coat or cutaway, which is part of morning dress or formal wear for daytime, is typically dove gray and worn with striped trousers. No matter the dress code, no man would ever substitute a black suit or a four-in-hand tie for the formal-wear essentials.

Nowadays, however, black tie has come to mean anything goes, which is a true tragedy in my mind. After all, a man can wear a suit and tie on any given day. But when an invitation calls for black tie, there is no wiggle room for translations. Even at the most formal of occasions, attendees sometimes show up in creative interpretations of the traditional look. But black tie always calls for a simple and suave uniform that never disappoints. The right tuxedo makes a younger man look more savvy and mature, while an older man appears undeniably stately in a great tux. The beauty of black tie lies in its simplicity, and guys have a foolproof road map to looking fantastic. All I can say is this: Gentlemen, please start your engines.

» *The right tuxedo makes a younger man look more savvy and mature, while an older man appears undeniably stately in a great tux.*

Gold and garnet cuff links and studs from Suzanne Felsen.

Style role models

A male style icon doesn't just flirt with a certain look. He courts it, ravages it, marries it, and moves on. Meaning, he commits to an image and perfects it before he reinvents his personal style with a fresh interpretation of fashion. The men I admire most stand out for wearing their personalities on their sleeves. Make those pinstriped sleeves.

Napoleon Bonaparte "emperor of flair"

THE
Historical Style

To call him a man in a uniform is a woeful understatement. This French revolutionary, known for his wrapped cravats, cutaway coats with tails, and tall standing collars, actually forbade women from wearing the same outfit twice to Court. (It was one of his sneaky tactics for boosting the economy.) He also decreed that military officials wear white satin breeches to formal occasions. Though he reigned in a period known for feminine flourishes like lace and embroidery, Napoleon always maintained a fierce virility. I love the bicorn, or two-cornered, hat he favored and his humble yet powerful "hand-in-waistcoat" stance.

IN HIS OWN WORDS:

"*A throne is only a bench covered in velvet.*"

"*A picture is worth a thousand words.*"

Oscar Wilde
"the poetic dandy"

THE
Historical Style

Never mind the fact that I share a birthday—October 16—with this suave Libran. It's his fondness for flamboyance that makes him my sartorial soul mate. Full-length fur coats, velvet capes, and patent-leather pumps were just some of the Irish writer's day-to-day staples. His appreciation for accessories must be noted, too. Wilde wore pocket squares, lapel pins, and even elaborate boutonnieres on occasion. He also loved velvet knee breeches, doublets, and cocktail rings, and he collected peacock feathers. Call him the ultimate Victorian fop.

<u>IN HIS OWN WORDS:</u>

"One should either be a work of art or wear a work of art."

"I have the simplest tastes. I am always satisfied with the best."

Cary Grant
"ever debonair"

THE
Historical Style

This icon of easy elegance inspired Don Draper's simple color palette and impeccably tailored style. Grant, a former stilt walker and juggler, knew every inch of his body and worked exclusively with a Savile Row tailor to highlight his trim physique. He often wore his shirt collars turned up to disguise what he perceived to be a broad neck—that's how attuned he was to his overall silhouette. In *To Catch a Thief*, he first appears in a striped pullover with a jaunty red bandanna at his neck and high-rise pants that emphasize his long legs. Hitchcock let Grant wear his own clothes because he so trusted the actor's sense of style. He once joked that he never dyed his hair because the stray grays that fell out matched his suits.

IN HIS OWN WORDS:

"My father used to say, 'Let them see you and not the suit. That should be secondary.'"

"Ah, beware of snobbery; it is the unwelcome recognition of one's own past failings."

Steve McQueen

"the urban outlaw"

THE
Historical Style

That glacial stare and cocky smirk may have been his best accessories. McQueen could make a three-piece pinstripe suit or a tartan plaid-lined golf jacket look gangster tough. Check out his Savile Row bespoke getups and gleaming Patek Philippe watch in *The Thomas Crown Affair*. Now that's a study in rugged sophistication. I love that he embodied masculinity with his penchant for Triumph motorcycles and racing cars. His preferred sportswear, from the leather bomber jackets to the Persol aviator sunglasses, always felt authentic to his rough-hewn lifestyle. He also popularized the turtleneck with sports jacket, one of my all-time favorite looks.

IN HIS OWN WORDS:

"I live for myself and I answer to nobody."

"There's something about my shaggy-dog eyes that makes people think I'm good."

Mick Jagger
"the rock-&-roll ruffian"

THE
Historical Style

With his whippet-thin frame and hip-slinging swagger, the Brit singer could easily moonlight as a supermodel. And any man who manages to look both macho and sexy entwined in a feather boa deserves a bow. Early on, he understood the appeal of a monochromatic slim-cut suit, and later he gravitated toward polka dots, stripes, and psychedelic prints that undulated with his every move. I applaud him for boldly accentuating his wiry stature with ultrafitted clothes like lace-up football pants, rather than trying to add bulk with pleats or boxy cuts.

IN HIS OWN WORDS:

"If I was starting out now, I would dress down but still hope to have some distinctive way of dressing down."

"Lose your dreams and you might lose your mind."

Lapo Elkann
"the suave scion"

THE
Historical Style

With his leonine mane, penchant for pocket squares, and perpetual bronze hue, Lapo Elkann personifies the aristocratic playboy to near parody. Case in point: This heir to the Fiat fortune and stepson of a Russian prince drives a two-tone blue Ferrari with a custom denim interior. He also has the Italian flag embroidered on the cuff of all of his dress shirts and has most of his suits made by a tailor in Turin. I love his sly dandyish way of pairing dinner jackets with denim shirts and Technicolor sneakers. He has absolutely no boundaries when it comes to his style.

IN HIS OWN WORDS:

"I'm crazy about pinstripes and vintage fifties fabrics."

"I need to make things mine. It annoys me to buy something that is imposed on me. I like shorter jacket sleeves and often fold the cuffs up. It's more modern that way."

Cocktail CHATTER

BLACK TIE ORIGINATED IN 1860 as an alternative to the more formal white tie with tails after a Savile Row tailor cut a short smoking jacket for the Prince of Wales. When a New Yorker named James Potter visited the English royal, he had a facsimile of the jacket made and later wore it back home in Tuxedo Park, New York.

MARK TWAIN HAD FOURTEEN WHITE LOUNGING SUITS CUSTOM-MADE, so he could wear a fresh one every day in his later years. He once said, "Light-colored clothing is more pleasing to the eye and enlivens the spirit."

BEAU BRUMMELL, the nineteenth-century fashionable dilettante, popularized the men's suit worn with knotted neckwear ensemble. He also stressed the importance of understated elegant silhouettes and tailoring. Best fun fact? The dandy reportedly took five hours to get ready and substituted Champagne for shoe polish.

CHECKLIST

Gently implore your date to dress traditionally for a black tie wedding and offer to help tie his bow tie.

Relay the ten essentials of a man's wardrobe to any male you know that doesn't yet own a suit.

Make the favorite man in your life watch these movies for style inspiration: *The Thomas Crown Affair, To Catch a Thief, Two for the Road,* and any James Bond flick. Take notes yourself for menswear-inspired silhouettes.

Give a guy a pair of cool, vintage cuff links, or a tie tack and show him how to dress up his look.

For God's sake, loan this book to a man in need. But be sure to get it back!

A
STYLISH
SEND-OFF

8

Fashion can be as fickle as a spoiled toddler. Hemlines suddenly elevate, polka dots become passé, and the designer "it" bag is deemed an "outcast" overnight. Pay limited attention to such caprices. I find it all to be amusing, actually. If you remain true to your own unique tastes and dabble only marginally in fads, your style will be both original and organic to your personality.

However, that style should always be evolving, too. Building on your look, even if it's a fairly new incarnation, will keep you inspired. That doesn't mean you must overhaul your closet every season. Rather, you want to add accent pieces and an investment garment occasionally to refresh your options and palette. Re-create that mood board every few months, too.

Maybe you recently experimented with new colors but have yet to dip your toe into florals or plaids. If you've mastered the two-inch wedge, perhaps it's time to graduate to a three-inch platform heel? Don't allow your style to stagnate. I am always on the lookout for a new silhouette or element of fashion that I have yet to explore. Make getting dressed and shopping an ongoing adventure.

Elisabeth Moss:
ON COLOR THERAPY

As priggish Peggy Olson, actress Elisabeth Moss rarely gets to indulge her ardor for feminine silhouettes. And her distaste for the color mustard is known on set.

"I love clothes. I love fashion magazines. I'm very much a girly-girl. The detail and care that women took with everything that they wore back in the sixties is impressive. You had the gloves, the hat, the bag, and the coat. I really like the fabrics and the buttons and those little details. You didn't just throw on jeans, a T-shirt, and flip-flops like you can today. At the same time, I'm very much a California girl. So I like my flip-flops and my tank tops.

"The clothes and the undergarments and the heels of the 1960s absolutely help you get into character. I don't think we could do our jobs as well without them. But that's speaking as the actor. Me, personally? I hate pantyhose, I hate girdles, and I hate wool. (Don't get me wrong: Spanx are great! But they are made of modern fabric.)

"The costume designer is sometimes the person who's closest to the actors. You deal with each other every day in a very personal way. One of the reasons that Janie is so good is because she takes input that we have as actors. She knows what she wants and she actually knows what looks best sometimes. She's so specific and detail oriented. I will try something on and think it looks totally fine, but she wants to change this button or make the collar slightly smaller. She's also just really fun to work with and makes me laugh.

"Janie is fashionable at six A.M. She will show up on set accessorized with a cute hat, while I'm in my pajamas and half asleep. I don't know how she does it. Maybe that helps her sense of detail as a costume designer. Plus it's not all Gucci and Armani and designer labels. She'll wear a great pair of designer jeans with a top from Forever 21. Style-wise, I definitely look up to her.

"The only outstanding argument that we have is her tendency to put me as Peggy in the color mustard, ever since season one. I wasn't the only person who noticed it, either. Other cast members noticed the exorbitant amount of mustard. Every time I see that color, I groan and we fight. Thankfully, in season three, she kind of gave in and I haven't seen it so much. But every once in a while she'll sneak it back in there.

"Hey, Janie: I like blue."

Christina Hendricks:
ON STYLE INSPIRATION

Every year, Christina Hendricks sees more and more women dressing up as office vixen Joan Holloway for Halloween. The actress, who dressed up to audition for the part in a snug sweater and sexy pencil skirt, understands the appeal.

"Clothes and style are hugely important. The way we present ourselves every day is so important and that image can change dramatically from day to day. It's amazing that *Mad Men* has had such an influence on culture and fashion. Certainly walking into boutiques and trying to buy a dress that makes me look like Christina and not Joan has become far more difficult in the past couple of years.

"On my first fitting with Janie, there was this full, full rack of clothes. And somehow, miraculously, every single piece on the rack fit me. Everything was gorgeous, too. I've never had that experience anywhere else. Janie had my measurements, like every costumer I've ever worked with, but she actually paid attention to it and got my body type right, too. It was a pretty wonderful experience.

"Working with Janie, I definitely have learned to open my mind to different silhouettes and different shapes. Not only that, but she really knows how to tailor to my body. That's so helpful. I never walk into a shop anymore and think, 'Oh gosh, I love it but it doesn't fit.' Instead, I think, 'I'm going to take it to a tailor and make it fit!' I have more fun shopping with friends, too. I'm always trying to convince them to try something new and if they say no, I say, 'You never know.' It's amazing how people will say no before they even try something on.

"My own style is a little romance and a little rock and roll. Ever since I was in high school—even a toddler—I've always been very much into feminine lacy, frilly dresses. But I didn't know how to do it right. I would have way too much lace or too many ruffles. I've learned how to narrow that gap. And Janie taught me to always show my waistline. That's one thing that I like about myself, so I should feature it. Every woman should show her waistline. Now I'm able to wear those romantic pieces, but in a tailored way.

"Sometimes I have to inspire myself by creating a theme. I went to a birthday party the other night and I was like, 'I don't want to go out. I don't even want to look at my clothes.' So I decided to get myself excited by dressing like a French jewel thief. I was being funny, but it also inspired me to create a look. I went for all black. I wore a cowl-neck coat with a beret and long gloves. Doesn't that sound like the perfect outfit for a French jewel thief?"

A pocket full of compliments

Do be a show-off about your new look. And no doubt someone—perhaps a co-worker, beau, or even your trusty dry cleaner—will notice those bold accessories or that chic red sheath. He or she may squint suspiciously and say, "Hey, there's something different about you." Or, better yet, gasp, "I love your look." Whatever you do, please don't swat the observation away like a pesky gnat at a picnic. Negating compliments is an utter no-no—and even an affront to the giver, who deserves to be validated for speaking up. Instead, be gracious and accept the praise with a simple "Thank you" and a big smile. Then bank that applause in your metaphorical "compliment account" because you may wake up one morning and need to withdraw it for inspiration. (You might even jot down that particular outfit in your fashion journal and note that it fetched some attention.)

Additionally, it's a wonderful practice to acknowledge someone else's style. I love to see the delight in a woman's face when her dress or shoes draw some words of flattery. The more specific the praise, the better. A compliment signifies that someone's efforts have been noticed. Hearing a simple "You look so great today" can uplift that person's posture and mood. Think of it this way: It costs nothing and takes but a moment to bestow a compliment. Plus that positive energy immediately creates a warmer atmosphere between two people.

Conversely, criticizing someone's style is akin to deflating a bicycle tire. My mother always voiced the old adage, "If you don't have anything nice to say, don't say anything at all," and I still dutifully follow it. You may not care for your friend's tie-dyed leggings, but you can certainly appreciate the fact that she's sharing a side of herself through her style. I'm always inspired by how my girlfriends put together their looks and I'm also appreciative of how their flair reflects their individuality.

» *Hearing a simple "You look so great today" can uplift that person's posture and mood. Think of it this way: It costs nothing and takes but a moment to bestow a compliment. Plus that positive energy immediately creates a warmer atmosphere between two people.*

My rule on rules

By now you have probably noticed that I don't believe in fashion dogma. After all, what I love most about style is that it allows you to express yourself. You can reveal your wit or nostalgia or sense of wanderlust through fashion. And please don't ever let me hear you moan, "But I have no style." It's in there, I promise you.

Having said that, I do have a couple of firmly held personal beliefs about looking and feeling great: First and foremost, fantastic style flourishes from a foundation of self-love. Remember those heart-thumping high school crushes that made you walk into walls? Well, now is the time to become infatuated with *you*. Buy a bouquet of Dutch tulips for your bedside table, dress up on a rainy afternoon just to admire yourself in the mirror. In short, pay more attention to yourself than anyone else every once in a while.

Second, always trust your own instincts about style. If you love a certain piece or color and it makes you beam, wear it. The confidence and exhilaration you exude in that outfit becomes a major percentage of your style. (Similarly, don't let anyone, from a salesgirl to a best friend, talk you into a garment that strips away your certainty.)

And, most importantly, always have fun with fashion. Look at cultivating your style as a creative outlet and indulge your inner fantasies.

As little girls, we play dress-up because we want to be someone else. Now we play dress-up to show the world the amazing women we have become.

PHOTO CREDITS

Page x: Kevin Winter/ Getty Images; Page xv: Moses Berkson; Page 8: Frank Ockenfels; Page 12: Carin Baer; Page 14: Top—Eugene Robert Richee/Getty Images, Bottom—Otto Dyar/ Getty Images; Page 15: Top—Eugene Robert Richee/Getty Images, Bottom— Eugene Robert Richee/Getty Images; Page 16: Bottom— Margaret Chute/ Getty Images, Top— Clarence Sinclair Bull/Getty Images; Page 17: Bottom— Silver Screen Collection/Getty Images, Top—John Kobal Foundation/Getty Images; Page 18: Bottom—John Bryson/ Time & Life Pictures/ Getty Images, Top— Hulton Archive/Getty Images; Page

19: Bottom—RDA/ Getty Images, Top— Hulton Archive/ Getty Images; Page 30: Frank Ockenfels; Page 38: Vintage ad, courtesy of Maidenform; Page 79: courtesy of Judith Leiber ; Page 112: Frank Ockenfels; Page 139: Frank Ockenfels; Page 141: Anthony Potter Collection/Getty Images; Page 154: Napoleon Crossing the St. Bernard Pass, by Jaques-Louis David/Bridgeman Art Library; Page 155: Hulton Archive/ Getty Images; Page 156: John Kobal Foundation/Getty Images; Page 157: Bob Aylott/Getty Images; Page 158: Anwar Hussein/Getty Images; Page 159: Scott Wintrow/Getty

Images; Page 164: Kevin Scanlon; Page 167: Brian Bowen Smith. Still-life images by Ryann Cooley on pages: xi, 2, 13, 33, 50, 51, 52, 53, 54, 55, 59, 61, 73, 75, 80, 86, 87, 89, 95, 101, 102, 113, 118, 119, 121, 125, 140. Page 174: photo of Janie Bryant is by Hussein Katz; photo of Monica Corcoran Harel is by Stefanie Keenan. Credits for the collage on page 175: 1. John Shearer/WireImage; 2. Charley Gallay/Getty Images; 3. family photo; 4. David X. Prutting/ PatrickMcMullan. com; 5. Amanda Edwards/Getty Images Entertainment; 6. family photo; 7. family photo; 8. family photo, 9. family

photo; 10. Larsen and Talbert Photography/Michael Larsen; 11. family photo; 12. Albert L. Ortega/WireImage; 13. family photo; 14. Michael Buckner/ Getty Images North America; 15. family photo; 16. family photo; 17. family photo; 18. "The Stylist Project" by Kimberly Brooks; 19. family photo; 20. Riverside Military Academy; 21. Moses Berkson.

ACKNOWLEDGMENTS

We're so thankful for the generous contributions of many people. As they say, it takes a village:

My delightful assistant Tiger Curran's great spirit, creativity, and fierce dedication to the project enhanced every page.

Immense thanks to Matthew Weiner for creating an amazing show that not only continually inspires me, but also influences the whims of current culture and fashion. I'm so grateful for our creative partnership.

Special thanks to Scott Hornbacher for all your gracious support of me and my dear department. Thanks, too, to Keith Addis.

For almost a decade, I have worked with the best in the business: Le Dawson and Joanna Bradley. The rest of my crew on *Mad Men* makes every day easier and better too. Special thanks to Lana Horchowski for her thoughts on getting pretty.

The loveliest of leading ladies—January, Christina and Elisabeth—bring joy and glee to my fitting room and provided awesome input for the book. Thank you also to the rest of the fantastic cast of *Mad Men*.

Wanda Soileau and her wonderful vintage shop Playclothes are a constant source of inspiration—not only to the look of the characters, but to my ever expanding personal collection, as well. Thanks for the wisdom.

Agent extraordinaire Maureen Toth: Thousands of thanks for a long, fruitful relationship and for always having my back.

Book agents Daniel Greenberg and Monika Verma of Greenberg/ Levine approached me with visions of a book and helped make it a reality, from start to finish.

Karen Murgolo of Grand Central took on this book with such warmth and exuberance. Best of all, she maintained that enthusiasm throughout the process. Thanks to Pippa White too, of course.

Our genius illustrator, Robert Best, brought verve, enthusiasm, and gallons of gorgeous to the book. Thankfully, I won't be calling you with any more changes!

Designer Eric Hoffman captured the vision, whimsy, and spirit of the project perfectly. His terrific eye for color, design, and layout makes every page a work of art.

Special thanks to Arthur Wayne and Brooks Brothers, Karen Valenti and Maidenform, Suzanne Felsen, Willy from Jezebel & Felina, Tracy Watts, Barton Perreira and the good people at Judith Leiber for their visual contributions.

For emotional contributions to their well-being, the authors thank their lovely families and friends.

Genius illustrations by Robert Best.

ABOUT THE AUTHOR

Emmy-winning costume designer *Janie Bryant* creates all of the looks seen on TV's *Mad Men*. She has worked on numerous films and TV shows. In 2005, she won an Emmy for her period costumes on HBO's *Deadwood*, and this year, she took home the prestigious Outstanding Costume Design award from the Costume Designers Guild.

Monica Corcoran Harel is a Los Angeles–based style writer who has reported on fashion and the culture of keeping up appearances for *InStyle*, *Variety*, *Forbes*, the *Los Angeles Times Magazine*, and the Style section of the *New York Times*. She also consults as a fashion expert for *Project Runway*.

1. With January Jones and Christina Hendricks at the Hollywood Style Awards, 2008 2. FIDM, 2009 3. Cuddling with Lucie, my gorgeous poodle 4. Hanging with the Mad Men *boys 5. The Costume Designers Guild Awards 2008 6. GranGran—Etoile Lillard Chesnutt 7. Laura, Mom, Paul, and me 8. Great Aunt Kate 9. My parents' wedding 10. Le Dawson and me at the 2005 Emmys 11. Paul Edwin Bryant II—my Dad 12. Having a minute with Matt Weiner 13. Partying with January at an Emmys bash, 2008 14. The Fashion File girls at the Costume Designers Guild Awards, 2010 15. Anna, Mom, Laura, and me 16. With Laura and Paul 17. Me with Pup at the Chateau Marmont 18. "The Stylist Project" by Kimberly Brooks 19. My first camel ride, in Morocco 20. Jim Watts and me at the Horton Society Dance 21. My backyard shoot for* Vanity Fair

HORTON SOCIETY DANCE

MISS JANIE BRYANT
and
CAPTAIN JIM WAT

HORTON SOCIET'
KING & QUEEN